D1494015

of related interest

Rehabilitation Counselling in Physical and Mental Health
Edited by Kim Etherington
ISBN 1 85302 968 8

Counsellors in Health Settings
Edited by Kim Etherington
Foreword by Tim Bond
ISBN 1 85302 938 6

Alcohol Problems
Talking with Drinkers
Gillie Ruscombe-King and Shelia Hurst
Foreword by Alex Paton
ISBN 1 85302 206 3

Addictions and Problem Drug Use
Issues in Behaviour, Policy and Practice
Edited by Mick Bloor and Fiona Wood
ISBN 1 85302 438 4

Understanding Drugs
A Handbook for Parents, Teachers and Other Professionals
David Emmett and Graeme Nice
ISBN 1 85302 400 7

Surviving Post-Natal Depression
At Home, No One Hears You Scream
Cara Aiken
ISBN 1 85302 861 4

Counselling the Person Beyond the Alcohol Problem

Richard Bryant-Jefferies

Jessica Kingsley Publishers
London and Philadelphia

First published in the United Kingdom in 2001 by
Jessica Kingsley Publishers Ltd
116 Pentonville Road,
London N1 9JB, England
and
325 Chestnut Street,
Philadelphia, PA 19106, USA.

Copyright © 2001 Richard Bryant-Jefferies

Library of Congress Cataloging in Publication Data
A CIP catalog record for this book is available from the Library of Congress

British Library Cataloguing in Publication Data
A CIP catalogue record for this book is available from the British Library

ISBN 1 84310 002 9 ✓

Printed and Bound in Great Britain by
Athenaeum Press, Gateshead, Tyne and Wear

Contents

To Stuart,
who helped me when I was younger but whom I
could not help because I did not understand
what an alcohol problem was

Acknowledgements

First and foremost I wish to acknowledge the clients with whom I have worked, who have brought me so much learning and who, in the final analysis, have been and are the true inspiration for writing this book. Hearing their experiences and their struggles, sharing in the process of formulating strategies for sustainable change, or simply being there with them as the one person who is listening, is a privileged position in which to be. My most important training ground has been, without doubt, the experience of working with *the clients themselves.* Without them, this book could not, and would not, have been written.

Whenever I have mentioned to people that I am writing this book, I have consistently received positive responses. Clients, professionals and friends have all commented that there is a need for a book to help people access ideas and informed perspectives on problematic drinking that draws on person-centred ideas and the experience of working with people who are affected by it. This has contributed to my perseverance in completing this book.

I would like to thank Tony Merry, Dave Mearns and Sue Wilders for their challenging and supportive comments on earlier drafts. I would also like to give thanks to Pippa Glassock, David Voyle, Patrick Coyne and the many others who have provided me with valuable feedback and encouragement.

Finally, I want to thank Lynn Frances, my partner, who has contributed not only her editorial skills to the production of this book, but also consistent emotional support, especially during my periods of self-doubt and of wondering if it would ever come together. Her ability to be touched by the content of the book, and her belief in it has been a source of encouragement throughout. Thank you, Lynn.

Note

The dialogues with clients in the book are fictional. Any actual words of clients are reproduced here with the permission of those involved.

Preface

I do not know what prompted me to apply for the post of Primary Health Care Alcohol Liaison Worker and Counsellor with the Acorn Community Drug and Alcohol Service in Surrey, other than that it somehow felt right. I had not previously had experience of working with people with alcohol problems. It was late 1994 and I had recently left my job as a Fundholding Manager at a GP surgery in Guildford, having earlier completed my diploma training in person-centred counselling and psychotherapy. I had chosen the person-centred approach because it offered me a way of working with people that made so much sense. My training reinforced my belief in the importance of having genuine respect for other people. I experienced the reality of the 'facilitative climate' through which growth can occur. I was fired up with the ideas of Carl Rogers, keen to apply them in my new career of counsellor.

It was while I filled in my application form that I knew it was the job for me. I had not previously thought of working in this area, yet looking back now I see that I owe a great deal to a past experience that I had thought was forgotten. Some years before, a manager of mine had had an alcohol problem and while aware of it I had no idea what to do, or how to help. The job application reconnected me with that experience. With hindsight, I could have done something. At the time, though, I was not in the right place within myself to offer anything; I certainly had no concept of how damaging and life-threatening a serious alcohol problem can be. He died and somehow the seriousness of his drinking did not impress itself on me until his locker was discovered to be full of empty sherry bottles. I think it is easy not to recognize a drinking problem sometimes, particularly when you enjoy a few drinks yourself.

My role at Acorn since 1995 has been to provide an alcohol counselling service to patients at a number of GP surgeries in south-west Surrey. It has been both a challenging and enriching experience. The challenges have been in the form of the settings (which are often not conducive to counselling), and the diagnostic emphasis that so differs from a purely person-centred way of working. The enrichment has come through working within a team of committed individuals and from the clients themselves with their diverse, and often traumatic, life-experiences, and struggles to change.

There has to be a belief within the counsellor that he or she can work with clients who have alcohol problems. There is a need for them to feel adequate to the task ahead. I have noticed how few courses training people in counselling and psychotherapy include modules on alcohol awareness and response. Dryden and Feltham (1994) have highlighted the need for trainers to alert students to issues concerned with working with problem drinkers. I am also struck, again and again, by the low expectations among professionals and volunteers of working with people who have alcohol problems. Yet with alcohol-related problems becoming a consistent and growing feature of our society, more and more health and social care professionals, and indeed everyone in the community as well, will find themselves having to respond to people who for one reason or another are demonstrating problems with alcohol.

Introduction

Alcohol use is a common enough feature of life at the beginning of the twenty-first century, as it has been for thousands of years. Most people enjoy the effects of alcohol, the 'oiling of the social wheels', the complement of a glass of wine with a meal, a few pints on a summer's day with friends in the beer garden or accompanying a few games of darts, that gin and tonic to relax at the end of a stressful day, or a relaxing of inhibitions so you can really enjoy yourself at a party. We like the 'loosening up' effect alcohol can have on us, the taste and the sensation of a pleasant glow in our throats and stomachs. However, for many this is not where the experience stops, or indeed begins. For them the urge to drink alcohol is overwhelming and the idea of cutting back or stopping is unthinkable or felt to be impossible.

Labelling

I have chosen the title for this book carefully. What has struck me most forcibly is the need to look beyond the labels attached to people and thus engage with the person himself. For instance, the word 'alcoholic' can bring up a range of images and thoughts:

- down and out
- sherry bottles in coat pockets
- having to drink every morning to stop shaking
- being unable to contribute to society
- being a waste of everyone's time
- being dangerous.

The label can create a barrier to seeing the person, making it difficult to acknowledge their potential, or achievements, their whole personhood. Added to this is the question of when such a label would be appropriate anyway:

- the professional drinking half a bottle of whisky or more a day to cope with pressure at work

- the company director daily consuming a bottle of wine plus gin and tonics while entertaining clients

- the single parent of either sex using alcohol to unwind and relax at the end of every day

- the sportsperson regularly celebrating successes with heavy alcohol use, or using alcohol to relax every time he steps out in front of 50,000 people.

Are these people 'alcoholics'? They may be unable to choose not to have their alcohol, yet they are far from the usual 'alcoholic' image many people have.

A label such as 'alcoholic' denies many other aspects of a person's life. It can certainly serve to obscure the recognition of an individual's uniqueness. I have sat in alcohol support groups struck by the rich diversity of skills, talents and experiences among those attending: professionals from all walks of life, people juggling work and a hectic home-life. Yet it is all too easy for someone to say they are just a group of alcoholics and lose sight of a greater reality.

The 'alcoholic' label can reduce any expectation of change. Maybe the person will not be able to change a drinking habit, maybe they will. Only time will tell. Being labelled 'alcoholic' can discourage some from trying, encouraging in them a sense of disempowerment, possibly exacerbating an already poor self-image. It can certainly be experienced as very judgemental. Having said that, many people see the label positively as a way of identifying themselves with a group within society;

this can strengthen their sense of identity and of not being alone with their problem. For many people the very fact of having a name for their problem can help them to accept it.

Not a simple disease

Over the years, an approach to treatment that is effective for all 'alcoholics' has been sought, but not found (Donovan and Mattson 1994). This probably stems from the general clinical view that specific diseases will respond to specific treatments and that, if you can find the 'right' one, you will cure the disease. However, the Centre for Research on Drugs and Health Behaviour (1994, p.1) suggests that 'no one approach to the treatment of alcoholism has been proved, by research, to be superior to any other for all problem drinkers'.

This is because we are not talking about a simple disease, rather a behaviour that has its roots in all kinds of emotional difficulties and distorted self-concepts stemming from conditional experiences, for instance, the negative and judgemental reactions of significant others, or significant losses and other traumatic experiences. Heather and Robertson (1989) suggest that problem drinking should be regarded not as disease but as a learned behavioural disorder. Problematic drinking can be a person's way of coping with a loss, or it may simply be a habit, the result of a heavy drinking lifestyle that is normal within a given culture. In Fossey (1994), Plant emphasizes that there are a number of factors that contribute to a developing drinking habit which include a whole range of social and environmental factors as well as the individual personality of the drinker, their genetic make-up and their unique life circumstances. Excessive levels of alcohol use have been identified as a 'maladaptive coping strategy' for dealing with stress and anxiety (Powell and Enright 1990).

The counsellor has to be empathic to the individual client's perception of, and the meaning they attach to, their use of alcohol. Each person has his or her own unique story to tell, and the role of the counsellor is to listen and enable the client to feel heard. We can sometimes overlook the power of giving someone time to be listened to; it is here that therapeutic contact begins, or is lost. Many clients using alcohol to cope with traumatic life-experiences have never before told their story, never been given the opportunity, or felt able to take the risk, fearful of ridicule and rejection, overwhelming shame, or simply of not being believed. I frequently find myself in awe of the experiences people have had, or are having, touched by the hurt and anguish present as they share their world. I find it very humbling, particularly when I have the sense of being the first person to hear a painful and difficult life-story.

Project MATCH

The increasing recognition that there is no single treatment that is the most effective, led to the development of the hypothesis that clients would do better if matched with particular treatments that addressed, and were better suited to, individual needs and characteristics. The 1994 Report to the Alcohol Education and Resource Council (UK) by the Centre for Research on Drugs and Health Behaviour (p.3) stated that 'we are still a long way from knowing whether treatment outcome can be improved by "matching" and which are the important "matching" variables'.

A call for further research led the US National Institute on Alcohol Abuse and Alcoholism to mount a large-scale matching study. Project MATCH[1] has been associated with an enormous amount of research, looking specifically at the issue of matching alcohol-dependent clients with three particular treatments: Twelve Step Facilitation Therapy (Alcoholics

Anonymous-based), Cognitive-Behavioural Coping Skills Therapy and Motivational Enhancement Therapy. One conclusion has been that they could all be helpful so long as the skilled helper was well trained to work within a clearly defined, structured framework.

On the surface, matching clients might be seen by some to be 'client-centred'; however, client-centred practice is not about how an 'expert' chooses a treatment for a client, but how the therapist and client work together and form a therapeutic alliance. This relationship is a key factor. How this may influence continuance of contact and outcome in relation to helping problematic drinkers is itself an area for further study, a fact also highlighted in the 1994 report. My focus is towards not so much *what we do* with our clients as *how we are* when we are with them.

Project MATCH is without doubt the largest research project on helping people with alcohol problems. With data still being made public, and papers continuing to be written, it is providing a vast amount of material to inform practice. It is a pity it only addresses three types of treatment.

Motivational interviewing

Miller, who has developed the 'motivational interviewing' approach to working with people with alcohol problems, suggests that confrontational approaches are counter-therapeutic and that the attributes of Rogers are really a basis from which motivational interventions should be developed (Miller 1985). In client-centered therapy confrontation is not used as a technique. However, the client will at times feel internally confronted by his own incongruence and anxieties as a result of experiencing empathy, congruence and unconditional positive regard being communicated by the counsellors. Motivational interviewing is an approach used widely in addiction services and is

> designed to help clients build commitment and reach a decision to change. It draws on strategies from client-centred counselling, cognitive therapy, systems theory, and the social psychology of persuasion. The appearance of a motivational interviewing session is quite client-centred; yet the counsellor maintains a strong sense of purpose and direction, and actively chooses the right moment to intervene in incisive ways. In this sense, it combines elements of directive and non-directive approaches. (Miller and Rollnick 1991, p.x)

Many would question whether this is truly client-centred, and I was among them until I met William Miller and was struck by his way of being and fundamental respect for clients. Now I would regard motivational interviewing as an application of a person-centred approach rather than a strictly client-centred therapy in the non-directive sense of Rogers.

Alcoholics Anonymous

A book written about helping people with alcohol problems would not be complete without mention of Alcoholics Anonymous (AA); it is such a powerful influence over people's thinking about alcohol problems. The Twelve Step programme, the participation in meetings and the support from 'sponsors' enables many people to take greater control over their lives. Counsellors and psychotherapists need to be aware of the Twelve Step process[2] as some of their clients will be using it.

It is enormously helpful that AA meetings are available, offering people the possibility of support on a daily basis. Some people choose to attend meetings simply as a way of breaking up a daily drinking habit, and/or for getting much-needed social contact. They are not so concerned with 'working the programme', and, while this can be helpful, the danger is that they remain at a stage that might be termed 'the dry drunk', not drinking, but not really changing. Others do change, working through the programme and at their recovery, and at playing an active part in the process of ongoing support and encouragement of others. Recovery is not just about not drinking, but is also very much about overcoming the emotional and mental attachments to an alcohol-centred lifestyle.

It seems that AA largely caters for those who are or have been at the extreme end of the drinking continuum. One criticism could be that it offers little in the way of preventive work, or of help to avoid developing a more serious alcohol problem at the point where alcohol use is only just beginning to generate problematic effects. Ward and Goodman (1995) comment that the AA message of abstinence is an extreme response to extreme situations. AA has three areas of emphasis that I have heard people indicate as being difficult for them to accept: adoption of the 'alcoholic' label; the use of language that implies 'alcoholics' are always 'in recovery'; the religious/spiritual angle within the Twelve Steps and the emphasis on a 'higher power'. Nevertheless, the fact is that AA helps many, and offers more in terms of availability of support on a 24-hour basis around the world than any other agency can hope to offer, but it is not for everyone.

Person-centred perspective

The key to the person-centred perspective on working with people with alcohol problems is that the focus is on the client, on the person him or herself, with the client having autonomy in choosing where to place the emphasis. It suggests that we are all subject to what Rogers termed 'the actualizing

tendency'. Bozarth (1998, p.6) describes this as 'the foundation block of person-centred therapy' and goes on to quote
Rogers:

> Practice, theory and research make it clear that the
> person-centred approach is built on a basic trust in the
> person ... [It] depends on the actualizing tendency present
> in every living organism's tendency to grow, to develop, to
> realize its full potential. This way of being trusts the
> constructive directional flow of the human being toward a
> more complex and complete development. It is this
> directional flow that we aim to release. (Rogers 1986,
> p.198)

The person-centred perspective emphasizes the client's potential to become a more integrated, satisfied and fulfilled person.
It acknowledges the client's unique heritage of experience and
identity. The therapeutic relationship in which empathy, genuineness and unconditional positive regard are present serves to
empower the client, as a person in his or her own right, to
make the choices that will enable them to have a more fulfilling
lifestyle. This generally involves resolving fragmentation
within the self and taking back control from external factors
such as alcohol through a process of developing greater integration and self-reliance.

Many problem drinkers, engaging in a person-centred relationship, can begin to gain a realistic sense of themselves and
unravel distortions within their self-concept stemming from
past experiences. Their alcohol use may be an expression of a
sense of self developed through negative or inconsistent conditioning, a way of dealing with feelings and anxieties that
have become established through experiences in life. It
becomes an expression of the person seeking to do the best he
can as he seeks to preserve an identity that is familiar to him
and that satisfies the conflicting demands of elements within

his self-concept. Many of the people I see with alcohol problems are experiencing low self-esteem and a poor self-image. The therapeutic process helps the person to feel validated and accepted. It can have an empowering effect with the person growing towards a greater realization of his potential as a person.

I would suggest that where a person can be engaged with in such a way that he can fully and genuinely explore his choices in life in a warm and accepting relationship, including his choice to use alcohol and its associated meanings and elements within his self-concept, then he is likely to choose to cultivate new habits and patterns of living, and develop a fresh self-concept that leads to less alcohol-reliance and greater self-reliance.

People need a range of options with regard to the forms of therapeutic support they receive and my experience is that the person-centred approach does offer a real opportunity for growth and alternative choices of lifestyle. It has application regardless of whether the client has a serious alcohol problem, is only beginning to experience problematic effects from alcohol use, or simply does not appreciate that his alcohol use is a problem.

Working with clients who are faced with the need to change a habit or a lifestyle can lead to the unexpected. Clients find themselves challenging attitudes and assumptions that previously were very much accepted and integrated into their way of being. Perceptions of past experiences are revisited and may be adjusted as feelings and anxieties are re-experienced in the context of the therapeutic relationship. The individual's sense of self can undergo tremendous shifts, and life can take on new meaning and fresh direction. For me, this is the attraction of counselling and, in particular, of working with this client group. The counsellor shares part of their journey into what can often be the unknown and the unexplored. It is a time of fear and hurt, of joy and creativity. It is not about finding solutions for people, but rather *helping to create the climate within which solutions may emerge.*

There is an ongoing debate within 'the world of alcohol counselling as to whether a professional counsellor who is *not* a recovering alcoholic can be truly empathic and helpful' (Feltham 1995, p.20). It can be valuable for someone to hear another's story, confirming his or her experiences. I have heard it said at alcohol support groups: 'I am here because the people here have had similar experiences'; 'I do not need to keep explaining myself. I can feel accepted for who I am'; 'Hearing someone else having similar struggles makes me feel less alone with my problems'. Yet in spite of this commonality, each person has his own way of interpreting experiences and shaping his sense of self and behaviour in response. Not everyone attaches the same meaning to his or her alcohol use.

In entering the client's world of experience, I endeavour to guard against making assumptions. A counsellor who has had an alcohol problem is challenged to hear the client's experiences and the meaning he or she attributes to them, and has to guard against believing that his or her own experience is also the client's. I have to be careful that my knowledge of the many psychological features that are common to this client group do not obstruct or distort my hearing of what the client is telling me. I myself have not had an alcohol problem, and have been virtually teetotal for the last decade or so. This was mainly due to finding that I had developed some kind of sensitivity to alcohol that left me feeling awful after just one drink. Yet my not drinking does not seem to be a problem in working with this client group. I may not have the actual experience of a drinking problem, but I am able to empathize with the thoughts and feelings experienced and communicated by my clients.

Aims of the book

While many of the ideas in this book are applicable for working with people who have other addictive problems, its primary aim is to help counsellors, therapists and all health and social care professionals to feel better equipped and more optimistic in working with people who have formed a problematic relationship with alcohol. Attitudes to working in this area of counselling are addressed. Particular issues concerned with problematic drinking among both young and old are considered, together with its effect on the family. The application of the person-centred approach is explored and what this particular approach has to offer the heavy or problematic drinker. The 'stages of change' model devised by Prochaska and DiClemente (1982), which is used widely in addiction services, is described. It offers a framework in which to work that I have found helpful. The attempt is made to demonstrate how the person-centred approach to counselling can be applied within this framework. Scenarios are given, together with sample dialogue to illustrate what can be offered. The attempt is made to help the reader appreciate a little more the world of the person with an alcohol problem, emphasizing that therapeutic bridges can be built and change for the better can occur, given the creation of a facilitative climate between therapist and client.

An important part of this book is the contribution from clients who express what they have found helpful and unhelpful from counsellors, friends and relatives as they have sought to come to terms with and resolve an alcohol problem. They also share what they feel society's view is of their plight. Some of these client perspectives have been written by people who use AA, and some by those who do not. Some accept the 'alcoholic' description, others do not. I value their courage in speaking out from their experience. It has been important for me that they should have their say.

The scenarios are fictitious yet drawn from the experience of working with this client group and the issues that arise. The names are fictitious and offered simply to provide a less impersonal sense of the client. My intention is to provide an opportunity to enter the client's world and be touched by what is said.

I am very aware of how little has been written on this topic from a person-centred perspective. Since developing my own speciality within this area, I often have counsellors contacting me, particularly from the person-centred way of working, asking what books are available specific to their approach. This is one of my motivations for writing this book. I remain convinced that the person-centred approach contains factors that are fundamental to enabling individuals to grow towards achieving more fulfilling lifestyles. I can testify, through my own practice, to the value of this approach, in helping people overcome problems associated with alcohol use. This book introduces the reader to the application of the person-centred approach within the work of counselling people with alcohol problems, and draws on other ideas that are widely used within the field of addiction work.

I am aware that some of what I say may not sit comfortably with everyone who describes themselves as 'person-centred' in their therapeutic orientation. Some will argue that they would not expect to raise the topics of alcohol use, relapse prevention or planning change, but would allow the client to introduce these themselves if they have relevance for the client's inner and outer experience. I also use words such as 'strategy', I talk of 'stages' of change that could be viewed as categorization, I offer ideas to clients that I believe might be helpful, and I have an agenda: to help people who are experiencing the problematic effect of alcohol use to reduce the damage they may be doing to themselves and/or others.

What I have realized through my work, and this is my personal view, is that while the therapeutic attitudes and values of the person-centred approach have much to offer this client group, other ideas can also be helpful. I hope that whatever occurs in my relationship with clients will prove to be enabling for them in achieving whatever they seek not only in the context of their alcohol use, but also in their own process of personal development.

One book cannot cover every aspect of the effects of alcohol and the ways of responding. The topic of problematic alcohol use is vast. This is not a medical book, or a treatment manual. However, it will equip professionals and volunteers who are called on to work with someone with an alcohol problem with a range of ideas and a framework within which both to build a therapeutic relationship and to offer the client the opportunity of developing and sustaining a less alcohol-centred lifestyle.

I hope this book will challenge you. I hope it will leave you more optimistic than before. Most of all, I hope that it will help all health and social care professionals to look beyond the alcohol problem to the person who, more than anything else, needs another human being to be a companion, someone who will listen to his unique story and help him face up to difficulties that previously only alcohol eased, and to accept himself in a fresh and more realistic manner. As Mearns and Thorne (1988, p.6) have emphasized:

> ... the client can be trusted to find his own way forward if only the counsellor can be the kind of companion who is capable of encouraging a relationship where the client can begin, however tentatively, to feel safe and to experience the first intimations of self-acceptance.

Then the client may begin to uncover their hidden potential for being human in a fuller and more satisfying way on the road to greater self-reliance, and perhaps in so doing gain a fresh perspective on their alcohol use and begin to make different choices.

Endnotes

1   For more information contact: National Institute on Alcohol Abuse and Alcoholism, (NIAAA), 600 Executive Boulevard, Willco Building, Bethesda, MD, 20892–7003, USA.

2   Alcoholics Anonymous World Service Inc. (1976) Twelve Steps and Twelve Traditions. New York: Alcoholics Anonymous World Service Inc.

CHAPTER I

Entering the World of Alcohol Use

I enjoy my work. It's hectic with deadlines and stuff. I really live for it. Alcohol is my only way of switching off. It works well and is not a problem. I arrive home late, carry on working, hardly get a chance to eat. Get through a few bottles of spirits a week, and some cans of beer. No problem. I fall asleep about 1am, then up at 6.30am. I work at weekends as well, when I'm not asleep. I think it's only the alcohol that's keeping me going. I'm a bit edgy sometimes late morning; a couple of lunch-time beers soon put me right though.

I just sit at home all day drinking – wine, vodka, whatever. Don't have much interest in anything, never have. Marriage is over. Don't see the kids any more. What's the point? Alcohol doesn't make me feel good, but it makes me feel better. Keeps me away from myself. Go without it? Piss off! It's what I do. I'm independent, won't let anyone near me ever again. People hurt you. I don't want to hurt any more. Alcohol's all I've got, my friend in a bottle.

As these two scenarios show, people are motivated to drink heavily for very different reasons. Both are problematic even though the persons themselves do not recognize this. Each is evidencing signs of dependence on alcohol to cope with very different environments, and within contrasting daily routines.

Both have at some point found alcohol to be a solution rather than a problem, yet it is now getting out of control. In my experience, people do not generally choose to have an alcohol problem; they make a choice to take alcohol because it is satisfying a need.

Making choices

It can seem that those who drink problematically are somehow different and that their choices and motivation are hard to understand. Yet we all make choices in our lives, and follow particular lines of behaviour, or develop certain habits. Why do we make a choice to do something? What does it give us? Why do we develop an interest in a particular activity?

A person chooses to join a health club. His or her motivation is to do something that helps him or her feel good at the end of a hectic day, or to relax and unwind. Someone else will join the same club, motivated more by the idea of social contact, joining with a group of friends, not wanting to be left out. For both people, the belief is that they will feel better from joining the club than not doing so. It is meeting a need.

Others make very different choices, shopping to relax and to gain a sense of enjoyment. The 'bargain hunt' gives them pleasure along with the actual buying of clothes that they really feel good in. For them, going home with that 'something for me' will lift their spirits. Shopping with friends makes it a social event, meeting another set of needs. Again, the choice is being made because it is experienced as satisfying by some part of their nature.

We fall into habits easily, continuing with our chosen method of gaining satisfaction and of feeling good. Why do we continue? First of all, because it works, because our choice gives us what we are looking for. It becomes part of our routine, a habit either associated with certain times or days, or in response to a particular set of feelings. In the above examples, the people highlighted would feel a little depressed or stressed if they were not able to make their choices. The thought of not going to the health club, or to hunt down that bargain, can leave them feeling empty, or more on edge than they might otherwise be.

If the health club closed, the person could react in a variety of ways. If it was their only social outlet, or a way of dealing with stress, they could be at a loss about what to do instead, which could trigger increased anxiety. One reaction would be to seek out another health club, to rekindle their good feelings by a similar method. Or they might feel very low, lose their motivation and spend more time at home, believing that there is little to relieve their social isolation or to get them away from the stress of the day.

The shoppers who can no longer afford the spending sprees may continue anyway – the 'feel good factor' outweighing any concern for the mounting debt. If they are told to stop, they might react angrily, affirming their intention to carry on, perhaps spending more, not wanting to be told what to do with their lives, or maybe seeking other methods of obtaining the items that they want. The idea of changing their routine might be too frightening to contemplate.

Others will accept their need to change, will be able to make a fresh choice and seek out something else that brings them a sense of well-being.

We carry powerful feelings towards our choices and our behaviours. We generally like our choices and are used to our routines. Usually people do not want to change unless it seems reasonable to do so and the change promises benefits over and above the current experience. Yet a lot of choices are the product of habit. Much of our daily routine can involve time spent on 'automatic pilot', not fully conscious of the choices we are making because, quite simply, we are doing today what we were doing yesterday, or what we always do.

While most habits can get out of control, not all are viewed as being so bad/dangerous or socially unacceptable as an uncontrolled alcohol habit. When alcohol gets into this automatic style of living, problems can arise and what seemed initially like a valid choice can become a regular routine with attendant risks of developing a range of problems.

People start to drink for a variety of reasons, which are generally similar to the reasons why any of us make choices. They divide into two broad categories:

- to gain something: confidence, 'feel good', reduced inhibitions, an image, enjoyment of the taste, social involvement, belonging and feeling a part of things

- to avoid something: pain (physical or psychological), memories, stress, responsibility, loneliness, people, or even oneself.

Enjoyment of the taste is a safer motivation than drinking for the intoxicating effect, particularly where this is a means of dealing with difficult experiences. It has been suggested that the only valid reason for drinking alcohol is 'recreation', and that you should 'never have a drink because you need one' (Cantopher 1996, p.127). Where the motive is experienced as an uncontrollable need then it is highly likely that a problem exists.

Why does the habitual drinker continue? As with other choices, they do so because it works, it provides them with a set of experiences they are looking for, it meets a need.

So what is the habitual drinker likely to feel if told he or she needs to stop, or cut back on his drinking? The reaction is going to be very similar to that of anyone else who is told to change something that is important to them: anger, heightened anxiety, feeling on edge, depression, nervousness, irritability, and generally finding it hard to settle.

For the dependent drinker, there are other factors that will motivate them to continue, for instance, clear signs of dependence when they stop, such as shaking, sweats and, in extreme cases, fits and hallucinations which can, if not treated, be life-threatening. Their experience will be that another drink makes them feel better, which it does – for them it is experienced as a solution rather than as a problem.

It is often thought that alcohol is alcohol, regardless of what form it comes in. However, I have heard people describe how they experience different behaviour triggered by particular drinks. It will vary from person to person. Someone can become fighting drunk on whisky, but simply extrovert on beer. Someone else will fall asleep on wine and slip into deep depression on drinking rum. Another will find spirits send them to sleep while wine makes them extrovert and bubbly. Taking alcohol is an intense experience for the body and the brain. Associations are established between feelings present within the person and the drinking experience: the alcohol content, the flavour, the particular chemical make-up of types of drink, and the setting in which alcohol consumption occurs.

Life as a motorway

An interesting image to reflect on is of life as a three-lane motorway: a slow lane (abstinence), an average-speed lane (safe drinking)[1] and a fast lane (heavy/dependent drinking). Everyone starts in the same place in the slow lane (unless his or her mother has been drinking heavily during pregnancy). During life, people change lanes. It is not always a case of an individual making a free and independent choice in this. Many factors contribute to acceleration into the fast lane, for instance, peer pressure, cultural or family norms and life-events.

On the motorway we can plot life experiences against drinking. While some people are abstinent all their lives and remain in the slow lane, others move into safe drinking as teenagers, increasing to heavy drinking during their early twenties, then reducing their drinking as they 'settle down' to a more stable lifestyle. Another person will have had a similar experience but have got into a heavy drinking environment (work or social), developing it as a central feature in their life. They continue in the fast lane with a high chance of health or other alcohol-related problems arising in their lives. Some gently accelerate through life, with an increasing risk of alcohol-related damage as they cruise into, and continue in, the fast lane. Others have been abstinent or in the safe drinking lane for most of their lives, and then, following a traumatic episode, possibly even very late in life, accelerate quickly into the fast lane. People can accelerate each time they are faced with a life-crisis or a significant loss and then ease back after a time, or when the situation has been resolved.

All who have accelerated into the fast lane do have a brake and may be encouraged to use it, returning to the middle or slow lane for the rest of their journey through life. Clients can understand their drinking pattern, and what it is related to, by plotting their drinking 'journey' against life events. This can reveal whether a person is at risk of developing a problematic alcohol habit to cope with particular types of life-experience, or whether their alcohol use is linked to environments in which they live or work. It is an idea that I am prepared to offer people, but only if it feels relevant to the client's interest, motivation and focus. Often it will be in response to a client voicing an interest in his drinking pattern and associations in the past, and how it has affected his or her choices in the present. I will remain mindful of the client's autonomy in choosing when and how they may wish to make sense of their alcohol use which I believe to be a crucial element of the person-centred approach to working with this client group.

When counselling from a person-centred perspective we have to be ready and prepared to accept the changes our clients choose to make, and to maintain our therapeutic presence alongside them. A key factor with the motorway image is that there is no 'us and them' in this model. Everyone travels the same road and we each have within us the capacity to change lanes in any direction. I think it is helpful and realistic to be aware of this. The fact that a client is in the fast lane may bring a particular set of challenges, but his world can be entered and understood. I will reach out to the breadth and depth of feelings that he is experiencing and endeavour to communicate my sense of what the client is experiencing. It can be a challenge to enter into the at times desperate and anguished inner world of the problematic drinker, to take the vital step of allowing 'us and them' to dissolve in the immediacy of the 'I–thou' relationship.

Multiple issues

I find that people with alcohol problems often have a range of issues that may become a focus for addressing. These may stem from early experiences, such as abuse (physical and sexual), emotional neglect, parents using alcohol problematically, losses of significant people, constant changes of home/schools, pressure to conform to family expectations; or more recent experiences, such as break-ups of relationships, difficulty having access to their children, unemployment, retirement, bereavement, general stress, violence. Some problems will be emotional/psychological, others will be related to environment and daily routine.

Jake's childhood was one of constant house moves, of never being in one place for more than a couple of years. He never managed to make and keep friends, and was never able to settle down. There were rows at home as well. He felt completely powerless and fearful of what would happen next. Nowhere felt safe. That first drink at 14 made him feel so different. He'd drink when he was feeling angry and frustrated. Arguments were normal for him and yet he also hated them. He yearns for a peaceful and settled life yet nowadays he provokes arguments at home so he can go out and get drunk.

Jake is split between himself as anxious, unsafe and frustrated, and as yearning for a more peaceful existence. He has a habit of argument and it has set up a pattern that is being carried into his adult life, making sustainable relationships very difficult, and bringing a high likelihood that the alcohol use may become increasingly problematic.

Clients may have a 'mental health condition', for instance depression, schizophrenia, mania or psychotic states. Some clients will self-medicate with alcohol (or with illicit substances or misuse prescribed or over-the-counter medication) to cope, often bringing relief to their symptoms yet complicating their condition. There is increasing emphasis on this 'dual-diagnosis' group in the UK. It has been suggested that up to 45 per cent of those diagnosed with mental health problems have substance misuse problems (ANSA 1997). In these instances counsellors who have not had relevant training are advised to consider referral on to psychiatric services for assessment. I think we have to be realistic. There are states of mind that are rooted in chemical imbalance that require chemical intervention. While this book has not been written to deal specifically with this group, many of the ideas regarding change and forming therapeutic relationships remains valid.

Jodie had heard voices in her head since she was 12. They encouraged her to hurt herself. She had always felt different, as if she stood out and was too visible to everyone else. She was sure they could all read her thoughts. Alcohol helped her to blank out the voices; it worked well for a few years but now she's even more aware of other people. They always seem to be watching her. Her paranoia is making it difficult for her to go out much. She is drinking all day to try to control it, but it is getting worse.

As Jodie continues to drink to control her problems, they are in fact getting worse. It is likely that she will continue with her alcohol use for it is all she has. However, the effects of the alcohol complicate her mental health condition. Medical intervention is required. It is a classic case of 'what do we control first?' While the increasing paranoia is an effect of her alcohol use, the actual origin of the drinking lay with the voices encouraging self-harm and an underlying mental health problem.

I find that there are two major factors present for many people with alcohol problems which make them particularly vulnerable: *sensitivity* and *loss*. Some seem to have been born with a hyper-sensitivity and have discovered that alcohol helps to cut down anxiety and emotional instability. Clients often say that they are extremely sensitive, easily moved to tears, and find it difficult to be with themselves when they are in an emotional state. The image I have is that emotions are like a jelly; some of us have emotions that are 'firm', others have emotions that are more 'fluid'. Emotional impacts cause the jelly to wobble. The more fluid it is, the greater the wobble. If the emotional jelly is firm, but keeps being impacted in one area, it gets 'bruised' and becomes less solid. Many people with alcohol problems have emotions that are either like soft jellies, or have areas that have been softened by impacts. Many people experience alcohol as numbing awareness of their highly reactive and sensitive emotions. For some, it seems as though it helps them build a protective shell around the damaged area, making it harder in later life to access or experience feelings. For others, alcohol enhances emotions. Clients frequently find this image helpful as they try to make sense of their inner world.

Physical and psychological dependency

The concept of dependence is frequently used to describe the relationship between the person and their alcohol use with a distinction then made between physical and psychological dependence (Royal College of Psychiatrists 1986). While some people will be psychologically dependent on alcohol in order to cope with certain feelings or situations, they may not have a physical dependence. Others will be physically dependent on alcohol as a result of continued heavy use (their bodies have adapted to the intake of alcohol to the point that there will be withdrawal symptoms if they do not drink alcohol); they may or may not have an underlying psychological experience of needing alcohol to cope with something. Let me illustrate this:

> Jack starts going to the local pub as a teenager and by the age of 20 is consuming an average of 4–5 pints most nights. Going out drinking is what his friends are doing and it is his social experience. A good night out is seen as feeling at least merry if not a little drunk. Gradually, tolerance develops and the 4–5 pints become 5–6 and later 6–7 pints each night to get the same effect. It is not a psychological prop, merely a habit that has now become firmly established as the 'norm'. Jack wants to continue to experience feeling merry or intoxicated.

In time, his body begins to adjust to the alcohol being present and wants more. There is a sense of a need to top up. The drinking in the evening begins earlier. Perhaps Jack starts nipping out to the local at lunch time, or having a couple of cans with lunch. He experiences shakiness if he does not have this lunch-time drink, it becomes a routine, a little more is needed, and perhaps the lunch-time session starts earlier. Jack is shaky in the mornings, a quick can before going off to work steadies things. If he goes without, he feels very shaky and sweats. He feels anxious, perhaps panicky, on edge and highly reactive. He has a drink and it all settles down; without it he cannot cope. He needs the alcohol to feel 'normal', to be able to function, to 'get up to speed'. He cannot contemplate going out without a couple of cans in his bag – just in case.

Jack has developed a primary physical/chemical dependency. There is also a secondary psychological dependency.

Robert, on the other hand, in his early teenage years experiences a traumatic loss of his father, and is unable to talk about this to friends or relatives. He is left feeling hurt and bitter about the experience, blaming himself for not 'being there' when it happened. His sense of self becomes undermined as he feels he wasn't good enough. He no longer sees himself as dependable, but sees himself as untrustworthy. As his self-belief begins to wane, he finds he is easily unsettled and has difficulty with self-confidence.

Robert happens to be feeling particularly low one day, walking home; he notices cans of beer on offer in the store on the high street. He buys a pack, not for any particular reason other than that they are on offer and, what the heck, why not try it out. Four cans later and he is feeling sharp and confident and ready to take on the world. He likes the feeling, and begins to develop a daily habit of buying his four-pack on the way home. Sometimes, when he is faced with a situation requiring a boost of confidence, he has an extra couple, just to set himself up. It works, every time. He can't believe it. He has an answer to his confidence problem.

So, for Robert, psychological dependence becomes established first. He discovers that the effect of the alcohol does not last. He decides he may need a stronger drink to 'feel good'. He checks the alcohol content and moves on to stronger cans; he finds himself drinking more, and throughout the day, to keep himself feeling 'good', keeping the feelings of low self-worth away. Soon, he is experiencing withdrawal symptoms if he does not have a drink and needs topping up early in the day. He has to keep drinking regularly to keep the shakes and the panics away.

For Robert, there is a primary psychological dependency with a secondary physical/chemical dependence.

If either Jack or Robert comes for counselling, they will present as being a dependent drinker, physically/chemically dependent, and with a sense that they need a drink to cope with life. Yet their histories are very different. On the motorway diagram, their paths will be similar, a steady acceleration from teenage years into the fast lane. However, the reasons are very different and plotting the acceleration against life events will clarify this. Jack began 'driving' fast to keep up with his mates, then he needed more 'acceleration' to get a buzz. He wants to maintain this exhilaration. Robert, however, accelerated into the fast lane for his own, internal reasons, finding for himself that it felt good to speed, it gave him a sense of power, of control, and he wanted more.

For Jack, changing the drinking pattern may be easier and more sustainable than for Robert because there is no deep-seated psychological dependence on alcohol. Jack has simply got into a habit that has led to chemical dependence. Change is never easy. However, if he can change his lifestyle, there is a good chance he can reduce his drinking and either remain a controlled drinker or abstinent if that is his choice.

For Robert, while he may change his drinking pattern, cut down, or even go through detoxification, it is unlikely to be sustainable if the underlying negative self-concept is not addressed, and his feeling related to the loss of his father addressed. The valuing process, the prizing unconditionally of the person through the therapeutic relationship is vitally important if reduced drinking or abstinence is to be maintained.

Robert's experience also highlights a common feature of psychological dependency. For a long time alcohol works, it anaesthetizes, boosts confidence and induces a sense of well-being and of coping with life. However, many people have commented to me on how fast it changes from being a solution to being a problem. 'I can name the day when it no longer gave me what I needed. I had more, it was all I knew, but it wasn't working. I kept drinking, convinced it would work again. It didn't, and never has since then. Now it only ever seems to cause me grief.'

Health risks of heavy alcohol use

Alcohol is scientifically known to be an addictive substance that, in sufficient quantity and over a long enough period of time, is likely to cause physical damage in the majority of people. It can generate diseased conditions or it can exacerbate weaknesses within the system. Much, perhaps most, alcohol-related morbidity and mortality occurs in people who do not think of themselves as having an alcohol problem (Royal College of Physicians 1987). Conditions that can arise from heavy alcohol use include: liver disease, stomach ulcers, oesophageal varices, heart disease and high blood pressure, cancers, pancreatitis, damage to nerves (peripheral neuropathy), diabetes, sexual and menstrual impairment, brain damage including alcohol dementia, Wernicke's encephalopathy (mental and behavioural change, paralysis of eye movement, unsteadiness) and Korsakoff's psychosis (profound impairment of short-term memory). A person's gait can be affected, not just from intoxication but because of damage to the nerves. Alcohol interferes with the absorption and use of nutrients from food. Heavy drinkers are often malnourished, particularly if they are replacing food with alcohol. As the body weakens people find themselves more likely to suffer from coughs and colds, to have muscle pains and to be generally listless.

Mood is affected, people often exhibiting behaviour that is not their 'normal selves'. For some this will be aggressive behaviour, for others it will be low mood, anxiety, depression. Alcohol is implicated in many suicides, used intentionally, to enter into a suicidal state, or unintentionally, leaving the drinker so low and depressed that suicide becomes a 'reasonable' choice. Alcohol blackout is common among heavy drinkers: it is not passing out but memory loss, for instance, being aware at 3pm of sitting in the pub having no memory of the past 36 hours. They have lived those 36 hours, but have no recollection of where they have been, what they have done, or with whom. I have seen alcohol blackout inducing a form of agoraphobia, because the person does not know whom they do not want to meet.

Many people at some level are uncomfortable about their drinking. They feel guilty and ashamed yet feel powerless to change, and drink more to protect themselves from these feelings. This can lead to secretiveness and denial that alcohol has been consumed even when it has. Even the person living alone may hide the bottles or cans almost as if they are hiding them from themselves, as well as from anyone who might visit.

People who are ashamed of their alcohol use and are experiencing a great deal of sensitivity can find themselves unable to cope with large supermarkets, open spaces, anywhere where they feel exposed, in extreme cases; this can lead to panic attacks and symptoms of paranoia. They find reasons to stay at home, partly to drink and partly to feel safe. As time progresses this can develop into agoraphobia, increased isolation and greater risk of health damage going unnoticed even when severe problems arise.

There are also the health-risks associated with withdrawal if heavy and prolonged alcohol use is suddenly stopped. This can bring on extreme shakes and fitting, *delirium tremens* and hallucinations and can be life-threatening. Detoxification from alcohol dependence needs to be monitored by either a specialist alcohol service or the GP. A client who is withdrawing from alcohol use in this way is in urgent need of medication and should be advised to contact his or her GP immediately. Failing this, they will gain temporary relief by taking alcohol; however, medical advice should still be sought.

People also develop tolerance to alcohol as a result of prolonged and heavy use. This, however, reverses when someone cuts back significantly or stops, and therefore a sudden return to previous high levels of alcohol use can be both dangerous physiologically and can lead to greater degrees of intoxication with increased risk of trauma following accidents.

Finally, there is the added risk associated with mixing alcohol with other substances, in particular, mixing alcohol with other suppressants such as heroin, benzodiazepines or methadone potentiates the sedative effects, increasing the risk of overdose or passing out and choking on vomit.

Use or abuse?

The title of this chapter uses the words 'alcohol use' rather than 'alcohol abuse'. This is because my sense is that it is not the alcohol that is abused, rather the alcohol is used to achieve certain experiences that are in some measure satisfying to the client, or are meeting a need. As a result the client may be considered to be abusing their bodies, causing damage to them, or exhibiting abusive behaviour towards other people.

Everyone who drinks alcohol uses it to a greater or lesser extent to achieve some kind of experience, yet society has generated an invisible line that we are not supposed to cross, a line that indicates whether our 'use' has become 'abuse'. In terms of health we have the safe drinking limits; however, as highlighted earlier, it is not necessarily quantity that defines whether alcohol use is problematic. Frequently it is behaviour that defines the line between what is and what is not a socially acceptable level. This, of course, may not match how the drinker views it.

The heavy alcohol user often does not know where the line is until he or she has gone across it. At that point he or she can become, in the eyes of society, less of a person and more of a problem. More and more people are crossing that line. It would help if the line could be made more visible, if the 'safe drinking' message were more explicit and more widely advertized, and if the glamour of high alcohol intake so prevalent on television and in other media outlets were balanced with images of the truly human tragedies that can flow from excessive alcohol use, and how it can affect anyone. People with no immediate history of alcohol problems in their family, and no previous heavy use themselves, can suddenly turn to alcohol during a crisis or a period of sustained pressure, leaving them surprised and perplexed if the use develops into a drinking problem.

Many diverse initiatives are occurring to endeavour to reduce the harmful impact of alcohol. It is not simply a reduction of all drinking that is required, but of the high-risk drinking (Stockwell *et al.* 1996). Unit labelling and warning labels on cans and bottles, appropriate training of staff serving alcohol, designing of safer pubs and bars, health promotion and education campaigns, control of availability, and increased taxes are among the many approaches that have been highlighted and researched (Plant, Single and Stockwell 1997).

We have today many outlets selling the addictive substance, alcohol – alcohol can get lost in all the talk around street drugs, when in fact it should be regarded not so much as a street drug as a 'high street' drug. Is it too simplistic to suggest that more outlets means more sales, means more drinking, means more harm and addiction, means more problems? People do need to be given the opportunity to make their choices about alcohol consumption based on clear and unambiguous information. However, society offers conflicting messages regarding drug use and it is in my view a sad fact that those working to help people with alcohol problems are in a growth industry.

As well as the health problems, the counsellor or other professional needs to be aware that problematic drinking can affect family life, causing disruption to relationships and harm to other family members – physical, mental and emotional: it can skew family finances, affect job performance (putting the drinker and maybe others at risk) and can lead to self-neglect.

It is not necessarily quantity of alcohol that is the problem: someone on low income may not drink very much, but it could still have a significant impact on the family finances so that food cannot be bought, or the quality of life for others is diminished. Is this truly an alcohol problem, or a socioeconomic one? Either way it is linked to the alcohol use, and the choices being made. The alcohol use may be recreational; it may be the one thing that can be enjoyed within an impoverished reality. From one perspective it is the human organism making a choice that enables the person to cope, to experience some good feelings, a sense of satisfaction. It is a positive factor. Yet it has a detrimental effect so it becomes a problem.

As we have seen, problematic alcohol use is often a symptom of deeper problems. Anyone who is in the habit of using alcohol to cope with life, or to face the new day, is still likely to be in need of something to 'lean on' if he or she cuts back. Hence the possibility that when people reduce or stop their drinking they will switch to something else. The smoker may need more nicotine. Often caffeine intake goes up. Other drug use (prescribed, over-the-counter or illicit) may increase to compensate. When a medication regime to support detoxification from alcohol is not carefully planned and monitored, there is a real risk of a dependency on the prescribed medication developing.

Facts and figures

So what are the statistics on the effects of alcohol? The following are taken from Alcohol Concern's (1997) *Measures for Measures: A Framework for Alcohol Policy* document.

- There are approximately 33,000 alcohol-related deaths a year in Great Britain.

- There were over 28,000 hospital admissions in one year (1994/5) due to alcohol dependence or the toxic effects of alcohol.

- About 65 per cent of suicide attempts are linked to heavy drinking.

- Alcohol is a factor in 40 per cent of domestic violence incidents.

- Alcohol is a factor in a third of child abuse cases.

- Offender or victim have been drinking in 65 per cent of murders and 75 per cent of stabbings.

This presents a grim picture. It is a huge problem, in both human and economic terms. Alcohol Concern also highlights the cost to society in financial terms:

- Alcohol-related problems cost British industry an estimated £2 billion a year because of absenteeism and poor work performance. (This figure does not include the 25 per cent of workplace accidents that are alcohol-related.)

- National Health Service (NHS) responses to alcohol-related problems cost an estimated £150 million per year.

- Drink-related traffic crime costs £50 million per year.

We can read the figures, say 'how terrible', 'something must be done', 'thank goodness I'm not like that'. Yet is the person with an alcohol problem really very different from anyone else? The answer is no, they are struggling with the same difficulties that many people face, but with the added complication of the alcohol use and its effects on the body's chemical make-up.

Client perspectives

Do you feel that society is largely sympathetic or unsympathetic to your struggle? Why?

'Unsympathetic as they think it is just a case of stopping, or drinking in moderation, and that it is *entirely* the fault of the alcoholic alone.'

'Yes, I think they are sympathetic, because they feel, "there but for the grace of God … ".'

'People don't want to know about the issue. The public avoids drunks and criminalizes them. You need to experience dependency to understand alcoholics. Alcohol is not given the attention that other drugs receive.'

'Society is very unsympathetic; they don't understand it is an illness and the mental condition that goes with it; you can't just stop, it's not a case of will-power.'

'I find that now, with more people in the limelight admitting to this problem, more people are beginning to understand the problem.'

Endnotes

1   UK government guidelines suggest that 2–3 units a day for women and 3–4 units a day for men, with no bingeing, is the safe drinking limit. Medically recommended limits are 14 units a week for women and 21 units a week for men. The more that is consumed above these limits, the greater the risk of damage to health. A unit is a single measure of spirits, a small schooner of sherry, half a pint of normal strength beer, lager or cider, or a standard glass of wine. Watch out for some of the higher strength cans of lager, or bottled ciders; some cans are 4.5 units. Volume in litres multiplied by the percentage of alcohol content equals the number of units.

CHAPTER 2

Alcohol in the Family

When considering families it is important to think in terms of 'systems' and 'the pattern of connections between one individual and another' (Street 1994, p.3) along with the meanings each individual takes from the family experience. This is certainly true for families that have been, or are being, affected by someone's problematic alcohol use. Family therapists make an assumption that 'if the individual is to change, the context in which he lives must change. The unit of treatment is no longer the person, even if only a single person is interviewed; it is the set of relationships in which the person is imbedded' (Haley and Hoffman 1967, p.v). While emphasis in the past may have been on categorizing 'the alcoholic family', there has been a movement towards a focus that is much more on family structure rather than the labelled disorder. From this, a perspective that is more all-embracing of the family can develop without the dominance of one individual's set of symptoms (Hoffman 1981). The emphasis is increasingly towards family structure.

This chapter focuses on the dynamics within the family in which alcohol has become a significant factor, and explores some diagrammatic images that can be helpful in understanding the effect alcohol has on family roles and relationships, and the difficulties that will be present for the family in returning to 'normal' if the problem drinker cuts back or stops. It then looks at two ends of the family spectrum: the young and the elderly.

In a functional family there is a general flow of responsibility from adults to children. In a two-parent family, the parents look after the children, providing a safe, certain and predictable environment. They also help each other with their various needs. The children will to some degree care for each other, generally depending on their relative ages although gender can also be a factor. This could be represented in the following way, the arrows indicating the general 'flow of responsibility':

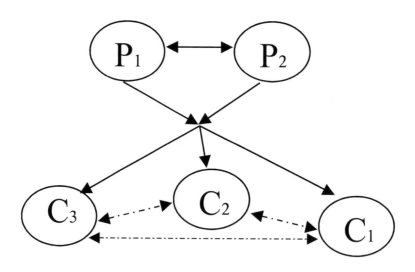

Figure 2.1 The flow of responsibility in a functional family

It is recognized that between 30 and 40 per cent of problem drinkers report at least one parent being a problem drinker (Velleman 1992). While it has long been thought that alcohol habits are passed on through the generations (Bleuler 1955) it may not necessarily be the parent's alcohol use itself that is the primary factor. Unpredictability and uncertainty from whatever cause are major negative influences on a child's development (Velleman 1993). Velleman and Orford undertook a study looking at the effects on 16–35-year-olds who were brought up in families with problem drinking present, as compared to those from families where this was not a factor. They found that it was not so much whether a parent or both parents had been problem drinkers that was the significant factor as a predictor of negative adulthood outcome, as family disharmony and the disruption and unpredictability of the parents' behaviour within the child's upbringing (Velleman and Orford 1993).

Unpredictability in early life

Some of the unpredictability associated with alcohol use by other family members can become the 'norm' for the child:

- Will I be picked up from school?
- Can I be sure that a promised trip to the cinema will happen?
- How will they react?
- Is dad going to be home for Sunday lunch?
- Is mum going to have my tea ready?
- If I invite my friends home, will mum or dad be drunk again?

Uncertainty can leave the child with a whole range of feelings that affect his or her self-concept. The child may blame him or herself, may believe he is not good enough or deserving of receiving what is promised. They may feel a lack of unconditionality in any love within the family, because the treats that would have made them feel special often take second place behind someone's choice to drink. This not only affects the child at the time, but will also establish a pattern for later life.

Effect on family patterns

Families tend to have certain routines and rituals that become the norm (Velleman 1992). Some may involve the use of alcohol, leading to a conditioning effect, for instance, always having a drink when there is sadness or anger, or to celebrate. The family may have an established pattern of drinking more on holiday, at Christmas or when relatives visit. Perhaps the family always offers visitors alcohol rather than tea or coffee.

Some of these are not in themselves problematic; however, they can become elements of a drinking problem. Family norms can be used to legitimize the drinking behaviour, the family system colluding to maintain the alcohol use even though the effects are disruptive and uncomfortable for all concerned. Co-dependency develops; the alcohol use and the adaptation and contributions of other family members to it set the pattern in a kind of behavioural and attitudinal concrete. Even though it can be extremely distressing, leaving family members struggling to support the problematic alcohol user, or giving up and blaming that person for everything that goes wrong within the family, the family system continues.

It is difficult for close relatives to begin to trust the problematic drinker, even when they are addressing their alcohol use. As one client put it, 'Lack of trust from my family in the beginning of my seeking help was difficult but understandable as I had lied about so many things for so long'. The family system is placed under enormous strain.

We can use the 'flow of responsibility' diagram to highlight how family members can be affected. The following examples are based on a 'two parents present' pattern. Diagrams can be generated to illustrate other family parenting patterns. They can provide a visual method of helping to make sense of some of the family interactions that shaped childhood experience.

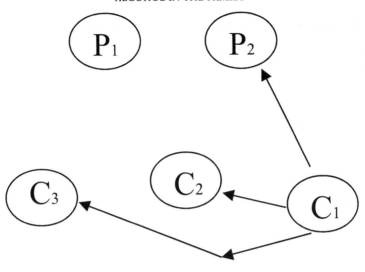

Figure 2.2 One parent drinking problematically, the other not coping; one child the primary carer

In Figure 2.2 we see a representation of the effect of one parent (P1) drinking heavily to the point of not engaging in family life, with the other parent (P2) not being able to cope with the situation and retreating from engaging with, and taking responsibility for, the family. The effect is that one of the children (C1), let us say the eldest, takes on child-care responsibilities as well as care for the parent who is not coping. The drinking parent is isolated.

A child is now at the hub of the family wheel, and is fast becoming an adult, being conditioned into taking responsibility for others. For some, this may become so established that in later life a choice of career is made in the caring professions. At some point, that child, as an adult, may reach a point of having had enough of caring for everyone else and always being the one who takes responsibility for others. The conditioned way of being can no longer be sustained and the person may enter a process of breakdown involving a reconnection to, or recreation of, a sense of self that is free of, or less subject to, the conditioning of having to be the 'forever responsible' person.

Another child may swing in the opposite direction very early on in adulthood, never wanting to be a carer again. It depends on how the child has interpreted the experience, whether or not the caring role has been absorbed as a satisfying norm and what impact it has had on his or her self-concept. Often the person who has experienced extremes in childhood will also swing into extremes as an adult: in this case, caring for everyone, or caring for no one. This will also impact on how much they are able to care for themselves, and their whole definition of what care means and what its boundaries are.

It will not only be the older child who is affected; all the children are learning about parenting in this situation. What lessons they will learn and how it will affect them in later life, only time will tell. To begin with it is likely that what they experience they will accept as normal, questioning this only if they have contrasting experiences. Yet even this can bring further difficulties as the child may well blame him or herself for what is wrong within their own family.

In Figure 2.2, the parent who is not coping is also losing self-esteem. Their mood may be low; they may feel they are letting others down, the children in particular. They will be left questioning their ability as a parent and, if that is their prime identity, questioning their belief in themselves as a person. This parent might turn to alcohol themselves to cope. Or they might adopt a strategy of drinking with their partner to try to help them reduce, which seldom works. They might seek advice from a GP, may be taking medication to address low mood, or be receiving counselling.

The problematically drinking parent may be quite oblivious to what is going on around them or they may be aware of it but find that the alcohol is so attractive to them and has become such a habit that they are unable to contemplate change.

Resilience to negative effects in children

There are important factors that help encourage resilience among children affected by disharmony in the family system. If only one parent is drinking, how the other parent responds and relates to the child is crucial. If he or she is able to provide stability and attention it can reduce the negative impact. Endeavouring to maintain a cohesive parental relationship, to present a united and caring front to the children can also help. If this cohesion is not possible, the maintenance of family affection and activities can reduce the risk of negative effects on the child. Finally, the stabilizing and consistent caring may come from another relative, a teacher, or a neighbour (Velleman 1995). It could be the counsellor or family therapist who takes this role.

When the drinking stops

Another perspective to consider is what will happen if the drinking parent stops drinking, or reduces and brings it under control to the point that he or she seeks to re-engage with the family. Will the children accept this? Will the responsible child be ready to let go of his or her powerful place, the taste of being an adult? Will the children be able to trust that it is a genuine change and that it will last? Will the other parent be able to move away from the low self-worth and also engage once more? Many relationships break down at this point. 'At least I knew where you were when you were drinking, on the couch every day; now you are out and about and I'm not used to it.' This can be particularly significant when the relationship developed and became established with problematic drinking already present.

The issue of co-dependency is powerful. The family system and the individuals within it may have become intimately bound to the problematic drinking behaviour. Having been established as the norm they adapt to it. Or the family system may have been 'alcohol-affected' from the outset. One family member may be actively encouraging another to maintain problematic drinking. Often the question of how alcohol is coming into the household will reveal who is enabling whom to drink. 'It's OK, when I feel in need of a drink my partner puts the money out on the sideboard for me.'

Family members may also sabotage someone's attempts to change. This frequently occurs when alcohol use is linked to power issues within a family. One person has power while the other is drinking heavily. As the problem drinker regains control other family members may do things that put him under pressure and lead him to relapse. Many family systems require a 'scapegoat': the drinker often fulfils this role as part of keeping the dysfunctional family system functioning. They may be pressured into it, or adopt it naturally having learned it in the past.

At the same time, the drinker can experience their own power within the family through their alcohol use; it can bring them attention and a sense of importance. Problematic alcohol use may be their way of maintaining contact with their self-concept of being a powerful factor, a significant person, within the family dynamic. Alternatively it can maintain a sense of being a nonentity, or a false sense independence and be a powerful way of not facing reality. Alcohol use has many roles and meanings, unique to each individual.

While a person changing their problematic alcohol use can place a strain on family systems, the change can have a positive outcome. Generally the problematic drinker themselves has to decide that they need help. Families can push, but this often leads to tension and arguments until the drinker themselves acknowledges a need for change. One client described it:

Only my family knows of my situation fully. Friends may guess but we do not discuss it. My family has given me support and purpose to pursue my goal of giving up drinking. The drinks cabinet is locked, bottles were marked, drink was discovered and thrown away. This did not make me give up but it kept the issue on the agenda! The real help came when I decided I wanted help. Until that point there were arguments and scenes but once I went to the GP for help, my family and I started working together.

Families may not always be able to make someone stop drinking who wants to continue, but they can certainly contribute to someone returning to alcohol use who is trying to stop or bring it under control.

Further family patterns

Let us briefly consider some more family 'flow of responsibility' patterns:

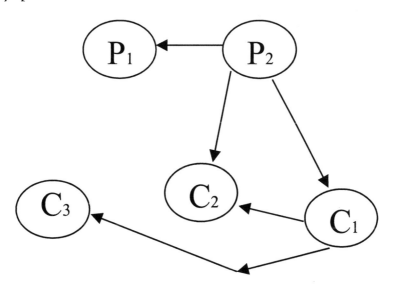

Figure 2.3 One parent drinking prblematically, the other in primary caring role with assistance from child

In Figure 2.3, one parent is drinking problematically (P1); the other parent (P2) is looking after him or her and the two eldest children (C1 and C2). The oldest child (C1) has been detailed to look after the youngest child (C3) and also to share in looking after the middle one (C2).

In Figure 2.4 there is a more extreme scenario with both parents (P1 and P2) drinking problematically and an older child (C1) having to take responsibility for caring for everyone and organizing a kind of chain of responsibility with the other children (C2 and C3).

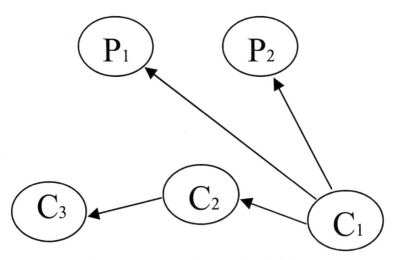

Figure 2.4 Both parents drinking prblematically; a child is the primary carer

Who is drinking problematically in Figure 2.5? This is a not uncommon situation. The father (P1) is drinking, is out at the pub most nights and is taking very little interest in the family. The mother (P2) also drinks although not regularly, generally in more of a binge pattern. However, she is left with the child-care responsibilities. When the mother does drink to cope with the pressures, after another row, or just to unwind from the demands placed on her, the children become a focus of concern: it may be so serious that they are placed on the

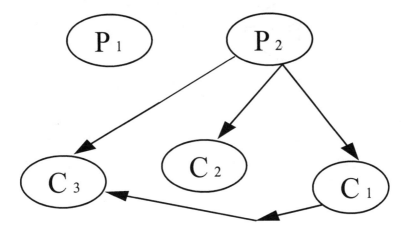

Figure 2.5 Both parents drinking prblematically; implications for child care

Child Protection Register. The mother feels a failure as the emphasis is placed on her alcohol use as the problem, and the father, as he heads out to the pub yet again, blames her for it all. The oldest child (C1) in particular looks after the youngest (C3) when the mother (P2) is drinking. In Figure 2.5, the periods when the mother is binge-drinking could be represented by dotted lines from her to the children.

It may not always be a parent drinking that is creating problems within the family. In Figure 2.6 the child on the right (C1) is the problematic drinker. The mother (P2) is taking responsibility for caring for everyone and is likely to be under a lot of stress. The father (P1) has had enough. The other two children (C2 and C3) are looking out for each other. Lack of support for the child from other family members contributes to him or her continuing to drink. This scenario can continue into adulthood with parents still divided over offering support, ensuring that the family fragmentation is further ingrained.

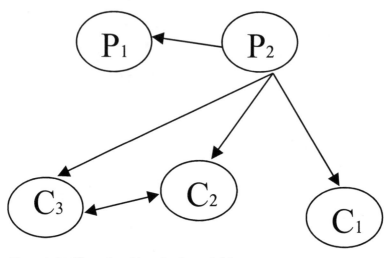

Figure 2.6 Effects of problem-drinking child

In my experience the attitudes and actions of family members play a significant part in enabling the problematic drinker to maintain a change. Where possible, couple counselling and family therapy have much to offer, providing opportunity for the relationships within the family system to adjust to change.

Client perspectives

What have you found helpful from friends, relatives or colleagues when seeking to overcome your alcohol problem?

'My *real* friends and family have put up with me and not given up and have always been supportive.'

'Support, understanding and, which is important, a feeling of admiration, which we all relish.'

'Being able to tell people how you feel and being able to trust them. By telling them the truth and knowing it won't go out of the room.'

'I don't have any old friends now, only new friends I've met since I've stopped drinking. My old friends were just drinking partners!'

What have you found unhelpful from friends, relatives or colleagues when seeking to overcome your alcohol problem?

'Knowing that my family drink, so when they know I am coming to see them they are still drinking in front of me.'

'Them telling me to stop drinking and not understanding that it is a disease just like diabetes, etc.'

'I think this mostly applies to younger addicts who are persuaded by their friends that a few drinks don't matter.'

'The friends who say you haven't had a drink for ... years, you must be able to drink now you are well.'

'Most people do not understand if they have not been through alcoholism.'

Alcohol and young people

For young people the immediate risk with alcohol is often the effect of intoxication rather than physical damage from sustained heavy use, although serious physical damage can still occur. Risks to younger people are likely to be from physical trauma through accidents, violence or, when inhibitions have been reduced as a result of the effect of alcohol on the brain, unprotected sex leading to unwanted pregnancy or the spread of sexually transmitted diseases. There is also a high risk of the younger person experiencing alcohol poisoning because, first, they have smaller bodies and the alcohol is less diluted in their systems; second, they will not have developed the tolerance to alcohol that many heavy drinkers develop; and third, they may have little understanding of the effect of alcohol and treat it like lemonade.

We are now finding alcohol problems in quite young children, with ten-year histories of problematic use before reaching 20. The risk of serious health damage to young people is very real.

Reasons why young people drink include: peer pressure, experimentation, coping with exams, difficult emotions and other life stresses (including coming to terms with adolescence), relationship problems, coping with abuse (physical, sexual, emotional) or an undiagnosed mental health problem, rebellion, family example, fun, to gain peer/street credibility, to be an adult.

All these can be reasons why adults drink as well. This can be used as a bridge to building understanding, particularly by an adult who is trying to help. Even adolescence as a transition experience has parallels with adults coping with stages of change in their own lives – new relationships or middle age, for instance.

Society does not serve young people well in preparing them to make informed choices concerning alcohol use. It is too available, often treated without respect and glamorized as an important feature of adult life. It is linked through the media and advertizing with images of success, sexuality, identity and of a 'feel good' factor. Children and young people are often faced with contradictory messages concerning alcohol, leading to confusion (Fossey 1994). Can the young person distinguish the image from the reality? A Home Office report (1993) recommended that 'café-style' premises should be introduced for families, the purpose being to try to demystify alcohol consumption and to weaken the link with adulthood while, at the same time, ensuring that the child's introduction to alcohol can occur in a more appropriate and trouble-free setting. Generating a perception of alcohol use as being a social experience with less emphasis on 'drinking to get drunk' would be helpful.

I think young people are more sensitive, both physically and emotionally, than adults give them credit for. This very sensitivity may cause them to start drinking to numb their feelings, then the physical sensitivity to alcohol may cause health problems. Within the adult world, everyone has a right to drink alcohol, but the child or young person also has a right – to be shown that alcohol has to be treated with respect.

Responding to the young problem drinker

Counsellors may have the young person themselves as a client, or a confused and concerned parent, unsure as to how to respond. The parent may experience panic, but this will not help. Key factors for parents responding to young people include:

- open discussion with their child

- taking time to plan their approach

- avoiding condemnation, to try to get alongside their son or daughter to understand their feelings and motivations

- being aware of the facts and having reliable information to hand

- setting a responsible example themselves – How is alcohol used in the family generally? What messages does the child or young person receive about alcohol?

- seeking a health check for their son or daughter when there is prolonged, heavy drinking

- looking for solutions within the family

- being prepared to contact local youth, alcohol or health services for further advice, information and support.

Working with young people requires sensitivity. It can be helpful if the younger person can appreciate that their feelings and concerns are being heard and validated, and that they are not very different from those experienced by others, for instance, the adult who is trying to help them. When a counsellor is involved they need to be sensitive to the young person's anxiety that nobody can begin to understand them and what they are going through.

Time can be spent usefully helping the young person to explore their needs and how alcohol seems to be meeting them; this can be contrasted with the disadvantages of alcohol use. An exploration of other alternatives may be necessary. Health implications can be discussed and the child can be helped to understand what health and well-being mean. Bear in mind, though, that young people often have a different sense of time from adults; the thought of basing decisions today on possible effects in future decades may not seem at all relevant to them. A 'here and now' focus that genuinely respects the young person's experiences is probably much more pertinent. It is vital that the counsellor has a clear recognition that, in spite of any problematic behaviour stemming from alcohol use, the younger person they are with has talents and potential that may be getting lost within the developing drinking habit.

A certain amount of heavy drinking takes place in college and university settings. Those who offer counselling in these areas are likely to be working with young people with alcohol problems. Some young people when they first go to college may not have had much experience of alcohol, and can do themselves harm. Or they may already be regular drinkers shifting up a gear within a heavy-drinking culture. By the end of a course extending over a few years, physical damage could have occurred. Young people in college settings should be encouraged to treat alcohol with respect. Sensitivity to the whole person coupled with having some ideas as to what might help to make changes in their drinking might make all the difference.

Many counsellors in college settings are familiar with issues related to heavy drinking through their client work. In this area of work there is a strong need for an appreciation of the effects of heavy or dependent drinking. An awareness of the importance of some of the strategies that a person is adopting when seeking to make changes, and why, will be helpful too. Often advice and support can be sought from local alcohol support agencies where situations arise that the counsellor is unfamiliar with.

We are also witnessing more concern over alcohol-related violence among young people. It is likely that in the UK the awaited national alcohol strategy will have an emphasis that addresses the need for alcohol policy to contain a strong social protection and criminal justice element. Whether this is the right emphasis will no doubt be a topic of much debate; however the fact remains that people are avoiding city centres at certain times because of the threat of alcohol-related violence. Counsellors working in agencies with young people need to feel confident and competent in working with those who are experiencing or creating problematic effects from their alcohol use.

Some of the young people that I have worked with really struggled to resolve an alcohol problem. Change often revolved around how much of their social lives − friends, where they met up − had become 'alcohol-centred'. Many felt as though they were swimming against the tide. I find myself again and again deeply touched by their determination to change in the face of enormous social pressures. The desire to be a part of things can be so powerful and yet there was also an awareness that for them alcohol use would lead them into trouble of one kind or another. I have worked with young people for whom alcohol use has been a way of releasing difficult emotions, gaining social confidence, finding their own identity, and witnessed and been part of their process in seeking out other ways of meeting these very human needs. I hope that future alcohol policy has sensitivity to the very human needs of some of the young people who get caught up in problematic alcohol use.

The problem drinking parent

A child or young person may be seeking counselling support because of the impact on their lives of a problematic drinking parent. As a result, they may feel guilty, convinced they are contributing to the problem, and needing to explore and gain a realistic perspective. It is likely that they will be experiencing a range of difficult emotions that they may not know how to handle. They will need to tell their story and feel it is heard. They may also need to consider strategies to deal with difficult behaviour by the drinking parent within the home. There may be violence, abuse, and/or neglect. There may be a need for other forms of support along with intervention from other agencies, particularly when they or others are at risk.

The elderly problem drinker

We are living in a time of an increase in the elderly population, whose health and social needs have to be catered for. Most of the current elderly population first encountered alcohol between the 1920s and the 1940s, a period of relatively low alcohol use. The depression meant there was not much money, and there was still a strong temperance movement influencing people's decision about whether or not to drink alcohol. Since then, alcohol use has gradually increased.

There are two groups of elderly problematic drinkers: early onset and late onset. *Early onset drinkers* began their heavy drinking early in life, out of habit or maybe to cope with a difficult event. What is important is that they have had a long 'drinking career' so the habit is well established. *Late onset drinkers* have been triggered into heavy or problematic drinking in response to a difficult experience late in life. This could be retirement or losses they have experienced, such as the death of a spouse or friends, or loss of mobility and independence.

Statistically, the early onset drinkers have more difficulty breaking the habit. It has become ingrained and may now be the only thing the person enjoys in life. It can be changed, but this is unlikely to be easy. The late onset drinkers have a higher likelihood of success in achieving a reduction.

Over the coming decades we will see not only an increasing elderly population, but also an increasing proportion of elderly, early onset drinkers, who began drinking after the 1940s, and established heavy drinking patterns early in life. This will place a strain on services to the elderly population.

Older people are vulnerable to the effects of alcohol because of the ageing process. Alcohol becomes concentrated within the body and therefore the risk of damage is increased. There is heightened risk of malnutrition, hypothermia and falls, and of adverse effects from mixing alcohol with prescribed and over-the-counter medication. It can affect the memory, depress mood and exacerbate degenerative mental health states. Alcohol also acts as an anaesthetic which can encourage many older people to increase their drinking.

Responding to the elderly drinker

The older problematic drinker has a right to information, advice and support. The 'it's all she has in her life', 'he hasn't long to live anyway' attitude offers nothing to the elderly problematic drinker. Creating an open relationship in which present difficulties can be discussed and the older person can feel he or she is being listened to and taken seriously has obvious therapeutic value. This may help them to question their drinking. It may be appropriate to point out that death from alcohol-related problems is not pleasant. Early onset, consistently heavy drinkers, by the time they retire, are highly likely to have a physical dependence on alcohol. It can require a great deal of support and encouragement to break the habit of a lifetime. Because elderly people often become frail, medical advice can be required if they are contemplating radical reductions in drinking.

Alcohol can be a means of dulling the discomfort of feeling useless. This can be particularly hard to bear for those who have lived an active life, perhaps in some profession in which their skill and knowledge drew respect from those around them. Now, having reached retirement and beyond, they can feel that nobody is interested in them. Many elderly people just want time, time to talk, to look back, to have interest taken in them. The counselling contact may be the one thing they look forward to: people generally feel more able to cope, and happier, when they have something satisfying to anticipate.

Reminiscence can help the elderly person feel valued. While this may play a part to begin with, I find that as a counsellor I need to watch that I do not get caught up in too much personal interest in the client's past experiences, colluding with this focus and denying to the client the possibilities that could emerge from encountering their current feelings and thoughts. It is important to offer the therapeutic encounter to the client's whole person. By enabling them to acknowledge in the warmth and valuing of the therapeutic environment the reality of their present situation, their fears of the future, there often comes a liberation to live a little bit more fully, and to experience themselves as more whole.

I find it helpful to explore with the late onset drinker what triggered the problematic drinking. The client is often aware of this. This may lead to planning alternative activities and interests – not to escape from difficult feelings, but to provide areas of life for the person to grow into. Engaging with the feelings within a supportive and therapeutic environment enables the person to gain strength to carry them and to begin to rebuild their lives.

I am convinced that counsellors can help elderly people with drinking problems as long as they are prepared to give time and remain patient with the client. The person-centred approach is particularly appropriate. In my experience, the person at a later stage of life can have high respect for the counsellor who is 'real' with them; they will value their readiness to try to understand their world and they will appreciate their being in relationship with them and having some degree of meaningful psychological contact. Probably more than anything else, they will appreciate being treated with respect, as a person in their own right. From this there is every possibility that the older person will reflect on the choices they are making, feel able to risk exploring their feelings towards their alcohol use and to contemplate the idea of change.

Living on the edge

Problematic drinking can have devastating effects on families, not only in the ways highlighted in this chapter, but also in creating divisions that become set in concrete over the years, with family members ostracized, others burning themselves out trying to keep someone together who is drinking heavily, or keeping a family functioning. Problematic drinkers develop behaviour that becomes 'normal' within their frame of reference, yet which is essentially adaptive in response to their formative experiences, and therefore may not match another person's sense of 'normal'. The following is an example of a conditioned sense of what is normal:

> I like to live on the edge, a bit of uncertainty and danger. The drinking is a big part of it, has been for a while. Gets me into trouble sometimes, a few trips to court, and that spell in prison, but that's part of it, isn't it? Life would be dull without a bit of excitement. I mean, it would be boring, wouldn't it? It was never boring at home when I was growing up: arguments, fights, all kinds of people passing through. You did what made you feel good. I still do. I don't do boring.

Among adults who experienced a disruptive childhood involving uncertainty, unpredictability, possibly violence or at least an atmosphere of aggression and threat, and often loss where they have felt unsupported, it is extremely common to 'live on the edge', to seek risk, excitement, strong emotions (highs and lows). I frequently encounter clients with a drinking problem who swing wildly from one end of the scale to the other. Like being on a see-saw (see Figure 2.7), they swing up and down. Sometimes thay may be at one end, sometimes the other, but it is always moving up and down where it is most exciting, risky and scary. There can be little sense of the middle ground, the point of balance. Things are either acceptable or not acceptable, with little scope for compromise. Although it is not uncommon for clients to dream of 'settling down', of finding some peace and stability in their lives, their attempts can be short-lived and unsustainable. Clients often experience this middle area as boring, unfamiliar to the point of alien, and not a place where they find it easy to be.

Another way of thinking about it is as a circle (see Figure 2.8). Here the risky area is on the edge, generally including the problematic alcohol use. I find it useful to introduce this imagery when working with clients for whom it seems appropriate as a result of what they have told me, and/or how I experience being in a therapeutic relationship with them. These images offer a framework, often enabling the client to explore what the edge is for them, both in the past and the present. It can also help them to consider what factors are currently present within their own middle-ground experience, and anything new that they choose to introduce. Time and

Figure 2.7 See-saw of feelings and risk

again I find clients responding to this image with 'Yes, that's me, always on the edge. I've never been in the middle'. Often a process of desensitization is required for clients to begin to

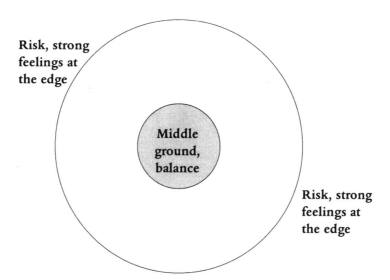

Figure 2.8 Middle ground

reject 'risky-edge behaviour' as their main source of 'feeling alive', and a resensitization in order to be able to accept new, self-chosen middle-ground activities, interests and behaviour as offering a fulfilling experience.

The person-centred therapeutic relationship offers scope for the client to experience not only the highs and lows in a climate of warmth and increasing self-acceptance, but also a great deal more, much of which will be new. Within the therapeutic alliance, all can be present including the middle ground which is explored at first tentatively. In time, clients become enabled to glimpse and develop a new self-concept which can inspire fresh patterns of behaviour, having integrated middle-ground experience into the range of what is normal, acceptable and satisfying to them. The following is indicative of the kind of realization I have witnessed people make:

> I always used to enjoy creative things, you know, making things. Yet the more I drank, the more boring those activities became. They didn't have the same buzz. Eventually I gave them all up. You know, I've just realized I've been carrying around this idea that they are boring ever since, even though I'm not drinking any more.

> I guess they were boring in relation to the drinking and everything that went with it. Now I get pleasure out of doing simple things. But I still slip back into thinking of my creative side as boring. I've left the alcohol behind but this idea is still with me.

Key points

- Alcohol can disrupt family systems.

- Unpredictability and uncertainty have a particular negative effect on children.

- Even when the problematic drinking stops, difficulties remain.

- Young people are particularly susceptible to the effects of alcohol.

- We can expect increasing numbers of older people with alcohol problems.

- People with alcohol problems often live at a 'risky edge'.

CHAPTER 3

Application of a Person-Centred Approach

In this chapter I am concerned with how a person-centered approach to counselling and psychotherapy can be applied to helping people with alcohol problems. It is my view that counselling and psychotherapy are interchangeable terms, particularly so in the context of the person- or client-centred approach. When a therapeutic relationship exists along the lines described in this chapter, personal growth occurs. This approach to counselling is much more about how the counsellor is with their client than what she or he does. It is fundamentally relational. Most psychological problems in my experience stem from relational issues, and most of these can be resolved through the creation and experience of healthy relationship enabling the client to redefine their concept of themselves. By 'healthy' I mean relationships in which the client is heard, feels understood, feels consistently valued as a person and experiences genuineness and clarity from the therapist.

Necessary and sufficient conditions

In a paper written in 1957, Rogers (1957, p.96) postulated that certain conditions, when present in a relationship, encourage growth. They provide what he theorized as necessary and sufficient conditions for therapeutic personality change. He described them as:

1. Two persons are in psychological contact.

2. The first, whom we shall term the client, is in a state of incongruence, being vulnerable or anxious.

3. The second person, whom we shall term the therapist, is congruent or integrated in the relationship.

4. The therapist experiences unconditional positive regard for the client.

5. The therapist experiences an empathic understanding of the client's internal frame of reference and endeavours to communicate this experience to the client.

6. The communication to the client of the therapist's empathic understanding and unconditional positive regard is to a minimal degree achieved.

In 1959, he shifted the emphasis by dropping the word 'psychological' within the first condition and suggesting that the need was simply for 'contact'. He also dropped 'endeavours to communicate' but rather sought to emphasize how important it is for the client to perceive the 'attitudinal experiences' of the therapist: empathic understanding and unconditional positive regard (Bozarth 1998).

The person-centred approach to counselling emphasizes the importance of unconditional positive regard, empathy and congruence as prime factors that will encourage therapeutic change within the client. These are now often referred to as 'the core conditions' although Rogers emphasized the six 'necessary and sufficient conditions' described above. What do psychological contact, empathy, congruence, unconditional positive regard and incongruence mean?

Psychological contact: For psychological contact to occur, both counsellor and client need to experience a sense of relationship, however minimal. This relationship requires a degree of communication which will often be in words, but will also be in facial expression, body movement, posture and the presence of quality attention towards the client. The client has to be touched within his or her own inner world of experience by these attitudinal conditions within the therapist. A sense of being together is present for both people.

Empathy: The counsellor is being empathic when he or she is accurately sensing what is present within the client's world of thoughts and feelings, and communicating this awareness back to the client in such a way that the client experiences being understood. The therapist is holding him or herself in accurate contact with the client's feelings and thoughts. The therapist feels free to move around within the private world that the client is presenting. Communication is sensitive to the tone of what is present for the client and what has become present for the counsellor through the relationship. While the client's words may be reflected by the counsellor, they emerge out of psychological contact with the client and a sensed experience of the client's inner world, not merely from a memory of what has just been said.

Congruence: When counsellors can truly be themselves within the therapeutic relationship, when they experience themselves accurately and bring an openness to their own self-experience, then they are being congruent. The words 'genuineness' and 'transparency' are often used to describe this state of being. The counsellor is not holding back on the client, the client is able to see the counsellor as he or she truly is within the relationship that is being created. This will lead to the counsellor voicing thoughts and feelings that are genuinely present within his or her awareness without pretences or defences (Mearns and Thorne 1988), bringing as much of their whole self as they are aware of into the relationship with the client. In therapeutic terms, the congruence of the counsellor's presence encourages growth towards wholeness in the client.

Unconditional positive regard: When the therapist experiences and offers respect and positive acceptance towards the client, wherever the client is in him or herself in that moment, and whatever feelings or thoughts are present and being expressed, and the prizing that is both felt and offered by the therapist is complete and not partial or conditional, then unconditional positive regard is present within the relationship.

Incongruence: Incongruence occurs when a person's interpretation of their experience does not match what has actually occurred. Conflicting and distorting elements within their process of attributing meaning to their experiences leads to them feeling anxious, and unable to be fully and accurately in touch with who and how they are. Their behaviour may not be appropriate to circumstances.

I find that the person-centred approach is challenging and demanding of me both as a person and as a therapist. When empathy, unconditional positive regard and congruence are present during a session, growth is much more likely to occur, yet to maintain all three throughout the therapeutic hour is, I would suggest, probably impossible. I do the best that I can, seeking to hold these facilitative attitudes as the client explores their inner world, describes their concerns, plans the week ahead, whatever they have need to bring into the therapeutic relationship at the time. It is important to emphasize that these attitudinal experiences (empathy, unconditional positive regard and congruence) need to be felt to be present by the client. The counsellor may register and understand accurately the client's feelings, and may feel whole and be transparent, and may hold within him or herself positive regard for the client, but for this to make a therapeutic impact it has to be communicated and this communication has to be received accurately by the client.

Counselling as a way of being

Empathy is not a skill, neither is congruence or genuineness, nor is holding unconditional positive regard towards a person. Empathy is a relational process between counsellor and client, while unconditional positive regard is an attitude held by the therapist. Congruence, in contrast, is much more a condition or state of being (Mearns and Thorne 1988). Together they form a way of being that lies at the heart of therapeutic relationship. They are innate potentialities that individuals can choose to develop if they so wish. They are facilitative attitudes that can develop as part of the process of personal growth and are deemed by the client-centred therapist as necessary and sufficient for promoting therapeutic change. To see them simply as basic skills is to miss the point.

For client-centred therapists, developing this way of being is a learning process, bringing greater self-understanding and awareness of their own world of thought, feeling and behaviour and enabling them to develop greater sensitivity and clarity in their relationship with others.

Tendency to growth

Rogers suggested that within the universe as a whole there is a 'formative tendency', and within each person there exists a tendency towards growth, what he termed the 'actualizing tendency'. 'Taken together', he wrote, 'they are the foundation blocks of the person-centred approach' (Rogers 1980, p.114). This actualizing tendency manifests through an impulse to grow towards realizing fuller potential as human beings. It drives the process of development and maturation by which the self seeks to be itself most fully.

In life, however, people experience negative conditioning or conditional responses from significant others (parents, relatives, friends, teachers, etc.) that can affect their self-concept. They can be left feeling threatened, unsure or confused, driven to express themselves in ways that are more to do with meeting the requirements of those around them than their own. They can feel unable to cope with certain experiences, perhaps having lost confidence when relating to other people; or they may have experienced abuse that has left them super-sensitive to hurt not only physically, but emotionally as well.

The urge to grow is still present, but potential for full functionality is reduced. It is as though this potential is buried beneath psychological defences, conditioned responses and façades that the person has developed in response to experience (Rogers 1961). When the presence of negative and conditional regard is being maintained, and the individual continues to live out of a negative self-concept, attitudes such as 'I am unlovable', 'rejection is normal', 'I can never be successful at anything' can take root. Experiences are symbolized to maintain these self-beliefs, contrary experiences being ignored or screened out for being inconsistent with the individual's developing self-concept or structure of self (Rogers 1951, pp.503–9).

These beliefs develop into 'configurations' (Mearns 1998, 1999) within the self-structure to become adopted as the person's reality. As they are reinforced, the person moves further and further away from an identity with their essential (organismic) self. They become increasingly centred in these 'configurations', creating patterns of behaviour, values and attitudes towards themselves and others that are either modelled on other people, or defences generated in the struggle to establish a self-concept and way of being that is satisfying. It is fundamental for a person to feel a sense of satisfaction with who they are.

I experience the actualizing tendency as an urge to be more fully and accurately myself, in effect to iron out the creases that my responses to negative conditioning have generated. It leads me to an increasing curiosity about myself: 'who am I?', 'why do I react to certain thoughts, feelings, situations in particular ways?', 'which configurations have I generated that provoke reactions that are not fully appropriate to the stimulus?', 'what is the basis for my own inner discomforts?', 'how can I enable myself to be more fully present in therapeutic relationship with clients?'

Effect of alcohol on development

Alcohol use is an experience that is symbolized by people. It does not always begin as satisfying; peer pressure may have influenced the person to 'introject' or accept a belief that it is worthwhile. Personal dissatisfaction with taste or feeling 'odd' from the chemical effect may be in conflict with the satisfaction that comes from sharing in the alcohol use, or whatever other meanings and experiences become present.

Configurations are accessed through alcohol use. When a poor self-image exists, alcohol can lower the mood in such a way that the feelings are exacerbated and confirmed. The configuration takes a greater hold on the person. Perhaps the person drinks in isolation, reinforcing a sense that he cannot cope with social situations. Or he has a powerful 'angry me' configuration that can live out under the influence of alcohol, bringing a sense of satisfaction to the individual concerned.

This can make them feel more themselves, yet it is actually enhancing incongruence, as the alcohol use is supporting the distorted self-concept that tells them 'I must take alcohol to cope with ... ', 'I'm a failure and alcohol helps me feel useless', 'I can only feel satisfaction with myself when I do things to make me the centre of attention'.

Alternatively, alcohol can bring experiences that challenge these configurations, 'I can be accepted by drinking heavily', 'I can be popular, the centre of attention', 'I can take risks which feel immensely satisfying because only risk can make me feel good'. Alcohol use can induce a new set of configurations almost as though the self is using the alcohol to fight back against negative conditioning: the individual derives a new sense of satisfaction from feeling confident, relaxed and socially interactive, giving them an altered self-concept – one that is rooted in the belief that alcohol is a necessity to maintain these satisfying configurations. It is then no wonder that later, when a person's heavy alcohol use is challenged, they react against it; it is simply too painful to countenance a change.

Alcohol use can also be a person's means of maintaining psychological contact with certain configurations of self; an example is someone who can only access and express sadness, or extrovert tendencies, through alcohol use. Seen from this perspective, it is possible that alcohol use is to some degree psychologically healthy as it helps the person to keep conscious contact with fragmented elements within their self-structure. However, it is a damaging method because of the chemical effect on the body.

Many clients who are using alcohol to cope with traumatic experiences, particularly but not necessarily early in life, may be experiencing 'dissociative states' and may be in what has been termed 'fragile process' by Warner (1991, 1998). A therapeutic environment is required in which the person can gently reconnect and reintegrate. The presence of such a state indicates that the client has experienced traumatic events generating a fragmented state of being in order to survive psychologically. My sense is that alcohol use can become in effect associated with an element within the person's dissociated state that cannot be heard. There is no pressure put on the client to connect with dissociative experience; rather they are allowed to find their own way into their individual awareness. Empathic sensitivity within the therapeutic relationship is vital in allowing the dissociated parts to be heard. It requires deep, relational engagement within the therapeutic climate to help the client slowly to reintegrate.

Impact of alcohol on the person

Through the person-centred alliance the client develops an increasing openness to experience (Rogers 1961). The impressions that impact upon him or her are experienced with reduced distortion.

> If a person could be fully open to his experience…every stimulus – whether originating within the organism or in the environment – would be freely relayed through the nervous system without being distorted by any defensive mechanism. (Rogers 1961, pp.187–8)

Alcohol suppresses the nervous system, hindering as well as distorting the free relay of stimuli. The body can discriminate between threatening and unthreatening stimuli without the person having awareness of the process (Rogers 1951). With alcohol in the system, impressions from surroundings can be misinterpreted. The person who is drinking heavily may have a distorted and reduced tolerance threshold to behaviour that irritates them, or which they misinterpret as a threat.

When alcohol is taken into the body, inhibitions are reduced first, then co-ordination is affected. Reduced inhibitions can free the person up to behave in ways that are in marked contrast to their normal behaviour. For some people this will be the great attraction, particularly when they need to face a situation that for them is difficult, perhaps a social encounter, or a tense relational problem. A couple of beers or a shot of vodka sets them up to face the situation.

With altered co-ordination comes altered communication. Reduced inhibition may have left the person communicating more than they might normally do, which means there may be greater transparency in their words, but as co-ordination is affected they may find it increasingly difficult to think clearly and to engage with the words that accurately reflect their thoughts and feelings. So, while initially alcohol might be said to enhance congruence in a certain sense in some cases, heavy use blocks congruence as the nervous/chemical system is disrupted.

There is a view that the fact of having alcohol in the body does not matter in terms of ability to be congruent, that a person is who they are regardless of the alcohol, and, if they are congruent to the chemically affected experience of themselves, they are truly congruent. In this period of history we are all more chemically affected than at any other time, when we take into account not only alcohol and drug use, but also chemicals in medication, foods and substances we make contact with, and pollution in the air and water. This leaves open the question of whether chemically affected congruence is true congruence, or a kind of false congruence. If the latter, can we ever regain true congruence free of externally introduced chemical influence?

Without doubt, alcohol can trigger personality change: people often comment that, since the alcohol problem got out of control, they feel they have lost contact with the person they once knew. 'It just isn't me. I want to rediscover who I am, but the alcohol gets in the way.' 'It sounds stupid, but it feels as though I lost myself somewhere, as though I got left behind.' The person they initially seek is the one whom alcohol helped to cope; however, sustainable change requires the client to look deeper, behind the alcohol-using configurations of self.

I find that one of the great challenges of person-centred counselling in this client group lies in creating a quality of relationship that is itself trustworthy enough for the client to risk some element of lack of inhibition without the use of alcohol within the session. When achieved, this is powerfully therapeutic, offering the clients a fresh and authentic experience of themselves that directly challenges their previous sense of self. Such reduction in inhibition is unlikely to occur when counsellor responses are of a judgemental or shaming nature (Farrell 1996). It is a sensitive time; the client can be easily discouraged if signals are given off that the client interprets as indicating that it is unsafe or that the therapist is unaccepting of them.

Creating the therapeutic climate

For me, the application of the person-centred approach is concerned with the creating of a therapeutic climate in which psychological contact exists and the core conditions are communicated, enabling the actualizing tendency to urge the individual towards fuller and more creative self-expression.

Rogers was very clear that people have enormous potential for growth and change. He wrote:

> Individuals have within themselves vast resources for self-understanding and for altering their self-concepts, basic attitudes, and self-directed behaviour; these resources can be tapped if a definable climate of facilitative psychological attitudes can be provided. (Rogers 1980, p.115)

Experiencing the unconditional support of a companion affords the opportunity for them to explore other ways of feeling fulfilled and complete. As with all my clients, I am required to cultivate empathy towards the inner, confused world of the problematic drinker. For this to occur, I have to be able to see and experience the client as a person beyond the alcohol problem, who is more than a set of alcohol-related behaviours. Miller and Joyce (1979) found that empathy of the therapist is a predictor of the client's drinking status at follow-up. Quality and accurately conveyed empathic awareness is a powerful factor in enabling clients to resolve alcohol problems.

When a client attends for a first session, and is unsure about whether or not they feel able to acknowledge having a drinking problem, the counsellor's quality attention and warmth will be powerful factors in building trust. I believe it is good practice to thank clients for attending, to empathize, where appropriate, with just how hard it has been to acknowledge an alcohol problem and then seek help.

To enable the client to confront their configurations and to recreate their self-structure, the person-centred counsellor is concerned with creating an environment in which the client can begin to accept themselves, with all their seeming contradictions and adaptations. Self-acceptance is a fundamental feature of human satisfaction. Acceptance of the configurations of self within the person-centred counselling relationship generates a healing process. Fresh perspectives can open up. Meanings can be redefined and experiences understood by the client in such a way that they become stronger to carry the hurt, or see through the self-doubt that has entered into their growth process. The individual is enabled to resolve psychologically the difficulties for which alcohol had been used chemically, or which alcohol use had induced and/or maintained. A lasting and sustainable change can result if any psychological basis for problematic alcohol use is undermined, and the client is enabled to generate and integrate a self-structure that evolves out of their experience of a person-centred therapeutic relationship.

The person-centred counsellor's willingness to be authentic within the relationship encourages this in the client as well. As the client risks greater self-awareness and finds it is acceptable within the therapeutic relationship, and begins to experience it as satisfying to them, they will move towards a clearer recognition and acceptance of the presence of incongruence: then they will begin to risk challenging it. Incongruence will at first loom large; greater discomfort is likely to be the result. Then it will begin to dissipate as re-creation and reintegration of the structure of self occurs. As the individual feels more complete, more able to engage with his or her whole self and to trust the prompts that emanate from it, they become psychologically free to express themselves in ways that are more responsive and appropriate to situations, enabling greater transparency, self-reliance and wholeness to emerge.

If the person-centred approach has a goal then it is surely to offer to the client the possibility of fuller functionality. What that will actually mean will vary from person to person: clients require the freedom to seek that meaning for themselves. Hence the importance of the therapist not directing the client into particular ways of being. It is for the client to choose freely and the therapist to trust that the client knows what is best and right for them. One of the elements of the person-centred approach that sets it apart is the fundamental theoretical position:

> that there is one central source of energy in the human organism; that it is a trustworthy function of the whole organism rather than some portion of it; and that it is perhaps best conceptualized as a tendency towards fulfilment, towards actualization, not only toward the

maintenance but also toward the enhancement of the organism. (Rogers 1978, pp.242–3)

Initial impact of person-centred counselling

Joan is an alcohol-using client with a negative self-concept: 'I'm not of value; I feel good when I'm drinking, and everyone thinks I'm great then, but I'm not really a person to be cared for.' She experiences in person-centred counselling that she is able to be valued and worthy of being prized as a person. For her, this is a direct assault on an aspect of her self-concept. Up to now, the heavy alcohol use is the only thing that has made her feel OK.

How might she counter this relational challenge to her self-concept and preserve her self-view? One way will be to stop seeing the therapist. Another way will be to increase the alcohol intake, and reinforce the configuration. The counsellor is challenged to accept that their approach may initially induce in the client a choice to take more alcohol. The effect of increased drinking will be to exacerbate the client's incongruence, maintaining the distorted configuration while pushing away any uncomfortable feelings about themselves. For Joan, things may well get worse before improving.

Another drinking client, Janet, has no distorted self-concept, or underlying emotional/psychological need linked to her alcohol use. She regards herself as a good enough person who happens to be a heavy drinker. She has no anxiety about her alcohol use. Her congruence means she may struggle to change her heavy drinking.

If there is physical damage from her alcohol use, producing messages to change in the form of physical discomfort or even pain, her condition becomes one of incongruence because, while her experience matches her self-concept and she communicates this, her body is undergoing damage which is not being linked to the alcohol use. Therefore incongruence is actually present within the functioning of the whole person. The counselling session may lead to greater discomfort for Janet as she experiences more fully the incongruence of seeking satisfaction from drinking while experiencing discomfort. Again, alcohol use could increase to block the tension that arises from this conflict within herself.

This kind of scenario will be encountered and counsellors need to be prepared for it. It is a paradox of working with this client group. This phase can be worked through and the consistent warmth and empathic sensitivity of the counsellor is vital. When I experience a sense that increased alcohol use is a possibility in response to a counselling session, I am likely to highlight this. I will seek to convey unconditional acceptance that the clients will make the choice they need to make, yet remain congruent to my sense of responsibility to the clients by offering them what is present within my own awareness. I see this as an expression of what I would term 'situational empathy'. I am sufficiently and accurately in touch with the situation, and with the client's frame of reference, so that I am aware of what could occur. I voice this, offering it from my specialist knowledge of the context, not from any sense of being an expert on my client. Not to do so can leave the client vulnerable and in danger of breaking contact at a critical time. Making visible that alcohol intake could increase as a result of greater awareness and experience of incongruence may enable some clients to come back who might otherwise have felt too ashamed by their reaction, or for whom excess alcohol might have sapped their motivation to persevere. To withhold helpful insight is, in my view, a form of negligence.

I find, as well, that it can be helpful to offer the perception to clients that they may feel 'woolly' and over-sensitive, that they need to take really good care of themselves, to take time to allow themselves to regain a grounded sense of self, particularly if this clearly has not happened fully during the session. I have had feedback along the lines of: 'You were right, I really had to look after myself and give myself time to adjust.' Time may even be given to planning how this might happen as a congruent expression of the counsellor's genuine and warm concern for the client's well-being. Otherwise, a client could use alcohol to get back to feeling 'normal', this could get out of hand and again contact could be broken. Not all clients anticipate the power and impact of a counselling relationship. While the counsellor trusts the client's ability to look after themselves, if the one resource they have is alcohol, then the whole issue can be voiced out of concern for the client's well being and made visible. I believe such a response offers a powerful message of warm and caring support towards the client.

Given that the person-centred approach is centred on the non-directive nature of the counsellor's relationship with clients, is highlighting the possibility that the client may feel worse before getting better, or may feel 'woolly' after a session, being directive? It seems to me that it depends on where the counsellor is 'coming from' when voicing these possibilities. Are they routine comments made to every client or a genuine response to the counsellor's experience of being in relationship with a particular client? I would suggest that when it is the latter the comments made are not being directive, because they voice of something which is produced by the impact of the client and their situation on the counsellor within the relationship.

Confronting drinking configurations

Mike has symbolized within his self-concept at an early age that he is unable to cope in groups or social situations. The following interprets a sequence of statements he might make during his life as his alcohol use develops.

> Stage 1: 'I'm 14. I can't cope with groups, never have been able to. Never know what to say, I just feel so awkward standing there. I find it hard to make friends. I am resigned to being on my own.'

Mike is already developing a self-concept as a person who is incapable of making friends or getting any sense of satisfaction or well-being from social situations. Awkwardness is his dominant experience.

> Stage 2: 'I started drinking at 16, I felt good, it gave me some relief from my anxiety and awkwardness at being out with groups of people socially. I still see myself as not being able to be social though. It seems nobody really cares about me very much.'

Mike is making connections between his alcohol use and his anxiety towards groups. He is finding a way to cope. He still has his poor self-concept in relation to social situations.

> Stage 3: 'Well, after a while it dawned on me that I was mixing more, and feeling more able to express myself with people, and make friends. Seems that alcohol can make you more attractive to people. I am everyone's friend when I'm drinking – it feels good.'

He has now identified alcohol as an extremely positive factor in his life. He has become the person whose sense of satisfaction is linked with alcohol use. He drinks more and more to maintain this experience.

> Stage 4: 'I'm 30 now, found a new partner last year. She is from a large family. We had a big gathering this last Christmas with her family, not much alcohol around though. I felt so awkward. I was terrified. I couldn't believe how bad I felt. When I got home I binged, I got really drunk. There was a huge row. I feel awful now.

She's threatened to leave if I don't do something about my drinking. I'd be alone again, maybe the best place for me.'

A significant life event has occurred that causes a break-through of awareness and sensitivity towards the feelings that alcohol has suppressed. If he turned to counselling at this point he would probably be confused, scared and wanting to know what to do. The crisis has presented an opportunity to explore what he is experiencing and to seek congruence, to be open to what is present within him and to recognize and experience that there is strength in this. At this point, three directions are possible.

> Stage 5a: The alcohol continues to be chosen to anaesthetize and satisfy the earlier established configuration concerned with being alone.

> Stage 5b: The alcohol continues to be chosen to enable him to make new friends and satisfy the configuration in which he sees himself as everybody's mate when he has had a few.

> Stage 5c: A definite attempt is made to accept the reality of the feelings he is experiencing in the present, recognizing it as a painful opportunity to confront his configurational tensions, and to look for a fresh way forward, possibly involving cutting out the alcohol.

In Stages 5a and 5b, Mike is seeking the security of familiar configurations and incongruence. In Stage 5c he is challenging these configurations.

Stages 5a and 5b are understandable. They would indicate that Mike is not able, at this time, to bring himself to confront his anxiety and discomfort. The facilitative attitude of the person-centred counsellor would be sending a powerful message to him prizing his worth as a person and challenging his self-concept and perhaps sowing seeds for the future.

Stage 5c would represent Mike's first difficult step towards a more congruent self-acceptance. To begin with he will experience increasing discomfort. The consistent warmth of the counsellor will offer Mike the opportunity to stay with this. The empathy and congruence of the counsellor will enable Mike to question himself and explore more deeply the incongruence within his inner world, offering the possibility for him to begin unravelling the configurations that have driven him towards his alcohol use.

One of the key elements of the person-centred approach to counselling is that it often generates within the client a state of 'dissonance'. They become increasingly aware of conflicting elements within their self-concept. Experiences of which they were unaware become present, introjections are revealed for what they are and the consistent unconditional positive regard of the therapist challenges the client's negativity towards him or herself. It provokes anxiety and discomfort that leaves the client struggling to resolve the tensions that arise. Two forces are at work, the urge towards greater congruence, and a reactionary urge to return to how things were (Mearns 1994). Holding the client within the therapeutic relationship causes a confrontation to occur. It is a critical time as elements within the client's self-concept, and the behaviours that stem from them, are weighed up and re-evaluated within the therapeutic relationship, offering the opportunity for constructive change to occur within the client's self-structure.

Congruence

Congruence is of particular significance to the inner process of the problematic drinker. It is concerned with the relationship between the human organism, individual awareness and the person's communication of their experience. When a person is affected by an event, is aware of its impact, experiences and interprets it accurately, and is able to communicate it in a manner that matches what is happening, congruence is present. There are no blocks or distortions in the flow. This can be represented by a triangle in which the solid line represents the free flow of experience (Figure 3.1).[1]

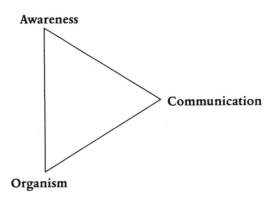

Figure 3.1 Congruence triangle (i)

We can use this model to represent congruence and incongruence within the client who is drinking excessively.

Figure 3.2 represents a person who is organismically in pain from alcohol intake – there may be actual physical damage, or

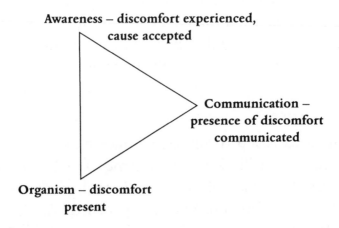

Figure 3.2 Congruence triangle (ii)

discomfort in feelings or thoughts. 'I know I've got stomach ulcers. I can hardly move some days. I want to get myself together again. I want alcohol out of my life.' The client is congruent concerning the effect of their alcohol use, being conscious of the damage and the reason for it and able to communicate freely their pain/discomfort, where it stems from, and their need to be pain-free.

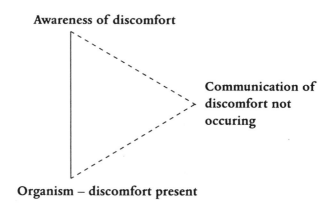

Figure 3.3 Incongruence triangle (i)

Figure 3.3 represents a person who is organismically in pain from alcohol intake – there may be physical damage, or discomfort in feelings or thoughts. The person tells the counsellor, 'I've a lot of discomfort in my throat, sometimes it feels so raw. And I've felt depressed. The doctor referred me to you for counselling for my low mood.' (They think, 'It's the alcohol, I know it is, but I feel so ashamed and I don't want anyone to know'.)

This client is aware that alcohol is the cause of their problems, and accepts this; however, they are unable to communicate their need for help for fear of the alcohol problem becoming known. There is incongruence, indicated by a dashed line in the figure. It is going to be difficult for this person to change at this point. However, if the relationship with the therapist is genuine, warm and accepting, the person may feel more able to verbalize their thoughts and be helped towards greater openness about their drinking. This often results in a greater readiness to change.

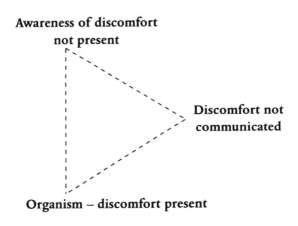

Figure 3.4 Incongruence triangle (ii)

In Figure 3.4 there is physical damage, but the person is unaware of it and it is not being communicated verbally or through behaviour. The client might be saying, 'I'm OK, I really am' (and thinking, 'I really am OK, in peak health'). This person is simply not consciously aware of the damage being done to their body because it has not yet triggered pain or discomfort. There exists within the person a state of incongruence.

In Figure 3.5 the discomfort or damaging effect of the alcohol is present within the person, and communicated through behaviour, but the individual is unaware that it is happening. 'It's good to be here and everything feels fine.' However, the client has forgotten they should have attended an appointment the previous week, and they are unaware of being two hours late for this session. Alcohol use has impaired memory function which is being communicated to the coun-

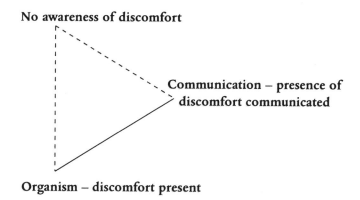

Figure 3.5 Incongruence triangle (iii)

sellor by the client's actions, but it is not something the client is linking to any alcohol-induced effect. Incongruence is present.

These triangles illustrate the situation for habitual, problematic drinkers with no underlying emotional issues fuelling alcohol use. However, when emotional factors are also present it is possible for the person to be congruent towards their actual drinking but incongruent towards their feelings or the configurations connected to the problematic alcohol use. The triangle becomes multi-layered.

In Figure 3.6, A–B–C can be thought of as representing an incongruent state when an underlying emotional trauma is unrecognized and uncommunicated, and alcohol is acting as an anaesthetic without 'conscious intent' of the person. Point A represents awareness, Point B the organism or body, Point C communication, each in relation to the emotional content. The triangle X–Y–Z relates to the physical problems stemming from alcohol use where they are accurately recognized, experienced and communicated.

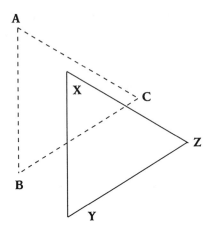

Figure 3.6 Emotional incongruence/physically congruent

Figure 3.6 might be summed up by a client commenting: 'I have to change my drinking. It's making me not feel myself. I get pain in my stomach sometimes that I know is because of the drinking. It's a habit I've got to get out of. It isn't doing my health any good. I'm sure if I get something to do with my time it will help.' However, this person actually began using alcohol a long while ago to cope with feelings associated with loss, and still does, but this is not consciously being recognised.

In Figure 3.7 we see a reversed picture in which underlying feelings are recognized, experienced accurately and communi-

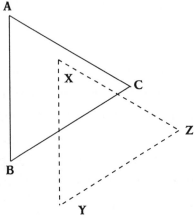

Figure 3.7 Physically congruent/emotionally incongruent

cated (triangle A–B–C); however the fact that problems which are arising are definitely alcohol-related is not recognized or communicated (triangle X–Y–Z). This client might say in relation to losing his job because his drinking caused him to be late: 'I feel so empty since losing my job, just because I arrived late a few times. I was tired. I cannot seem to find fulfilment in my life. Still, having a few drinks helps, always has. I may feel a bit dazed sometimes, but that's not a problem, I never get into trouble.'

There are many different triangular relationships that could be formulated to reflect more of the whole person. People carry with them areas of experience and expression that are congruent, and others that are not. Can a person ever have complete congruence across all aspects of their experience as a human being? Is full functionality a genuine possibility, or a potential that we inevitably all fall short of? It seems that full functionality as a person might always be limited. There are so many signals passing through the human central nervous system which we are not conscious of and yet which are part of our functioning as human beings. The counsellor may never be wholly congruent, but can be sufficiently so in the context of what is being disclosed by the client. When this is the case the potential for growth is present in the moment. One key aspect of person-centred working is that the primary reality is the moment-to-moment, person-to-person contact and relationship between counsellor and client.

From the client's perspective, it is important that the counsellor is a competent human being who is prepared to give time, to listen, to hear, to be non-judgemental and to be authentic. 'Can I be good enough?' is a question Rogers is said to have posed, and it captures a quality of humility and willingness to self-question that is vital to this approach.

I find that the issue of congruence and incongruence is a major factor when working with this client group. I watch clients realize they can trust me with facts about themselves, or their drinking behaviour, that previously were left unvoiced, or communicated as half truths. 'I'm OK. Up-and-down week, you know. I'm not drinking too much now, certainly less than I used to', becomes, 'Not feeling too good about it. A bad week. Not a full bottle of scotch a day, but at times it was over half a bottle.' It can be painful to admit some things not only to others, but also to ourselves in the presence of another person. I believe that being sensitive to this, and allowing the client time to come round to greater openness contributes to a fuller and more helpful therapeutic relationship.

Avoiding the 'expert' trap

Person-centred counselling requires me to treat every client as unique in order to enter fully into relationship with them, and to see them as the experts on their own lives. The counsellor's ability to be freely and openly in relationship with the client is more important than a knowledge of alcohol and its effects in terms of building the therapeutic relationship. However, when an alcohol counsellor is offering an assessment, or making decisions as to the client's physical or mental health and whether other forms of treatment are required, then knowledge of alcohol and its effects are obviously important. If a client requests particular information that the counsellor has, then it seems appropriate to give it. However, in client-centred counselling, the therapist aims to minimize the power differential within the relationship rather than take the position of all-knowing expert, offering scope for the development of greater client autonomy.

> *Client:* Well, you're the expert, you know what is best for me. You tell me what I should do about my drinking.

Counsellor: You really want some direction. I certainly have some knowledge of alcohol and its effects, and ways of promoting change, yet I am interested in what you would like to do.

In this example, the client's need for direction and expert advice is accepted, yet they are offered the opportunity to describe their own goals and hopes. The direction of the session is put into the hands of the client. The hope is that in time the client will realize that they hold the final power to make change, and that the counsellor's role will be to support this, offer ideas that might be helpful and encourage them in reaching their goals.

However, it does raise an important issue, and for me it comes down to defining roles and responsibilities. As a counsellor working within an agency set up to help people resolve problematic drinking, I am likely to offer 'specialist' knowledge on the topic. My role gives me this responsibility. Yet I am not going to offer 'expert' knowledge on the client. Clients are the experts on their own lives and experiences. I see myself as applying person-centred counselling principles within a particular specialism.

Self-disclosure of a drinking problem

Disclosure or non-disclosure by the counsellor of a drinking problem needs to be considered. Some clients are very clear that they need to know if the counsellor has ever had a drink problem. The application of the person-centred approach requires transparency. Some counsellors may have given up drinking because of its effects:

Client: So, did you ever have a drink problem?

Counsellor: I had to give it up many years ago because I was getting instant hangovers and I think my body was experiencing its toxic effect.

Client: So you don't drink now?

Counsellor: No.

Client: I really wish I could do that.

Counsellor: You really feel that strongly about being alcohol-free?

This can allow the client, should they wish, to engage more fully and deeply with their experienced need to be alcohol-free. Or they might find this too threatening and engage with their need to be a controlled drinker. It will lead to an exploration of their feelings, motivations, hopes and fears. The dialogue might develop in a different way:

Client: So you don't drink now?

Counsellor: No.

Client: So you don't really know what an alcohol problem is?

Counsellor: Only the problem I just mentioned. I sense it is important for you to feel understood.

This is the counsellor responding honestly to the question posed, yet also reflecting an underlying concern within the client that they feel to be genuinely present. It would only be an appropriate response if the concern for the client's need to be understood was present in the counsellor. It has to be authentic. It could be that the counsellor senses the client's wish to be with someone who has had a similar experience. This will then be voiced: 'I am experiencing a sense of your wanting to be with someone who understands from the standpoint of having been there.'

Of course, the counsellor may not have experienced an alcohol problem and might respond to the initial question with: 'I have not personally experienced an alcohol problem'. The danger would be to say then 'but I have worked with a lot of people who have problems so I know quite a lot', immediately claiming the expert position at a point when the only expert in the room on the client's problem is in reality the client themselves. The counsellor might usefully add something which would emerge from their experienced wish to understand their client: 'Maybe I can learn how it has been for you?' or 'I'd like to understand how it is for you'.

The client will feel understood not by claims of being 'expert', but by the nature of the responses to what they say and how they feel, within the counselling relationship. It is my experience that a counsellor does not need to have had an alcohol problem to convey an appreciation of what a client is describing and for the client to feel heard and understood. However, as with all clients, the counsellor has to be attentive and sensitive to what is being made present within the therapeutic relationship.

The client may feel strongly that they can only be understood by someone who has had an alcohol problem themselves. This view should be respected. Referral on to another counsellor may be necessary. Yet problematic drinkers are all unique, each has a personal reason for drinking, each has their own set of life experiences. Similarities in the client's story to the experience of a counsellor (personal or through work with other clients) can get in the way of the counsellor's moment-to-moment attention to what the client in front of them is saying and experiencing. Other relationships/experiences may give the counsellor clues as to what may be present for the client, but that is all. The client's story is theirs alone and needs to be heard.

Where the counsellor has experienced problematic drinking themselves they might respond to the question, 'Did you ever have a drink problem?' with a simple 'yes'. Depending then on what the counsellor is thinking and feeling a further comment may be added:

Counsellor: I am wondering what significance that has for you in our relationship

or

Counsellor: I am also aware that while there may be similarities, your experience is unique to you.

The extra comment will only be made as a congruent expression of the counsellor. What I think has to be avoided by the counsellor is excessive and irrelevant personal disclosure. The counsellor is there to engage with the client in their world, to help them feel heard and understood, appreciated as an individual within their set of life-experiences.

As the counsellor is allowed the opportunity to enter the private world of their alcohol-using clients, they will soon realize how much pain and self-doubt is often concealed behind the alcohol barrier. Entering those inner worlds, understanding why alcohol has been chosen, can leave the therapist convinced that, given similar circumstances, they too might have made the same choices. Truly to enter another's world of alcohol use, or any private world of pain and hurt, can be a sobering experience (pun intended).

Client perspectives

What have you found helpful and unhelpful from counsellors when seeking to resolve your problems with alcohol?

'The fact that counsellors don't judge you, accept you for who and what you are, help you to rebuild your confidence in yourself.'

'I find a balance between one-to-one sessions and group work ideal for me. I have learned to talk to others about how I feel, within a caring environment. I feel that unless you are willing to talk truthfully about how you are feeling and what you have experienced then counselling will not work for you. It has taken about 18 months to understand why I drank – it is a long but worthwhile process.'

'Until my most recent counsellor, all the counsellors have said basically "just stop drinking" which was no help at all despite having a very supportive GP.'

'They listen to you rather than telling you that you are not right.'

'None have been helpful until recently. My current counsellor never told me to stop drinking; suggested three-quarters alcohol to one quarter something non-alcoholic, never set a time scale and said take it in your own time. Gradually with the help of medication and a good GP, and my counsellor, I was able to go from three-quarters of a glass of alcohol topped up with a non-alcoholic substance, to 50/50 to 25/75 to no alcohol and 100 per cent non-alcoholic drink.'

'Their ability to listen, give support and help, and help take away the sense of shame which is with most of us.'

'It may have been helpful to have more counselling in the early, difficult stages.'

Key points

- Counsellor empathy, congruence and unconditional positive regard experienced by the client are fundamentally therapeutic.

- Individuals are subject to an 'actualizing tendency' towards fuller functionality.

- Conditional experiencing distorts growth.

- Congruence is open and accurate experience, awareness and communication.

- Alcohol generates incongruence, distorting the flow of experiencing within the person.

- Congruence of the therapist is a crucial factor in encouraging greater congruence within the client.

Endnote

1   The congruence/incongruence diagrams included in this chapter were previously published by iUniverse.com in a collection entitled *The Person-Centred Approach: Applications for Living*, edited by Doug Bower. We would like to thank iUniverse.com for permission to reproduce them in this volume.

CHAPTER 4

The Cycle of Change

The 'Cycle of Change' model was formulated in the 1980s to provide a framework for working with smokers (Prochaska and DiClemente 1982); however, it has become more widely applied to people with addiction problems. With few counselling training courses including much on alcohol counselling, and alcohol problems affecting so many people, the need for counsellors to have some framework for working is crucially important. Some may argue that from a strictly person-centred perspective other models are unnecessary; however, the cycle of change as I apply it is not so much a method of working but rather a framework for understanding which can inform the therapeutic process. It provides a way of making sense of change, of where people are within that process, and what is most likely to be helpful to the client. It can also help the clients themselves to appreciate their own process. Figure 4.1 is an adaptation of the original model.

The model suggests that in relation to change people will pass from one stage to another. What are the elements of change that might be experienced by the client? The client may:

- be in a state of not wanting to change or seeing no need to change (pre-contemplation)

- be thinking about change (contemplation)

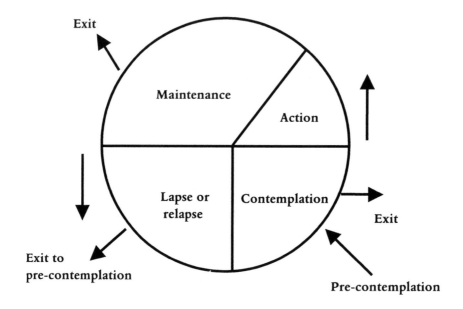

Figure 4.1 Cycle of change

- ○ be actively planning a change (contemplation)

- ○ have considered change and decided not to (exit from contemplation)

- ○ be putting a plan of change into action (action)

- ○ be maintaining the change (maintenance)

- ○ no longer be thinking about the change because it has become an established part of his or her life (exit from maintenance)

- ○ have relapsed on change and gone back to the way they were, but feel uncomfortable and still want to change (returned to contemplation)

- ○ have lapsed on change, but then re-established the changed behaviour (returned to maintenance)

○ have relapsed to the point of having given up, be no longer thinking about change and denying any discomfort about it (exited to pre-contemplation).

Pre-contemplation

This stage is representative of the person who has no wish to change; it is not on their agenda. In terms of alcohol use, they are denying that they have a problem, are not aware of the problem, or a problem simply does not exist. To try to push a person into change that they do not regard as necessary is unlikely to be very helpful, and is not person-centred.

Problematic drinking is often meeting a set of needs. When a person finds it difficult to recognize or admit to having a problem with alcohol when in reality problems are occurring, or are threatened, this difficulty may be the product of a number of factors: a genuine belief that they do not have a problem, a fear that they will be labelled 'alcoholic', a fear that to admit to the problem would mean change that is too frightening to contemplate, a poor self-image that leaves them feeling they would be unable to survive their problem becoming known by others or a profound sense that they are not worthy of being helped.

Where do congruence and incongruence fit in with this stage? As a counsellor I am endeavouring to be sufficiently self-aware and empathic to sense the presence of incongruence within the client and to voice it. This could take the form of information known by the counsellor about the effects of alcohol that are not known to the client. I have no problem offering information that is relevant to the impact alcohol seems to be having, or is likely to have. I have specialist knowledge and am not going to deny offering it to the client. My congruence might also take the form of expressing my awareness of contradictions in what the client is saying, yet in a manner that reflects an acceptance of what is being experienced and communicated by the client. The communicated congruence of the therapist is a powerful feature of therapeutic change, often enabling the client to engage with discomfort about their drinking problem. As inner tensions become more visible to them there comes the possibility of moving towards accepting within themselves a need to consider change.

I find that it is also important at this stage to convey to the client that, should they choose not to consider change, or acknowledge a problem where one exists, the door is open for them to explore it further at a later time. Warmth and acceptance are conveyed. When this occurs within an ongoing counselling relationship it will be left for the client to reintroduce the topic, unless the alcohol use impacts significantly on the therapeutic relationship leaving the counsellor with a need to voice congruently what they are experiencing.

Contemplating change

Here the client has begun to own their discomfort about their drinking. It could be that they are now aware that it is having a negative impact on their lives, or on those close to them. Some other life event may have occurred to make them question the amount they are drinking: the death of a friend linked to alcohol use; a health problem of their own that is clearly alcohol-related; a drink-driving offence.

At this stage, the client wants to explore the issue of their drinking and whether it is a problem, to understand why they drink and what they might do about it. There are some helpful tips for enabling the client (and the counsellor) to gain insight into the drinking pattern. From a person-centred perspective it is important that these are offered and not set as a task that the client has to complete. The most widely used is the weekly drinking diary in which the client records significant factors related to their drinking pattern such as: how much they drink, how much they spend on alcohol, time spent drinking, when and why the drinking started, how they felt before and after they drank, where they were when they were drinking, what else they were doing at the time and how other people reacted.

Not all diaries are as comprehensive as this, and not all clients will want to fill them out. Some will find it difficult to complete a diary – often a factor can simply be feelings of shame about what they are consuming. It may be that the family does not know and they are afraid of someone finding it. Avoidance is not necessarily an indicator that the person does not want to change.

The diary can be a start to help the client gain insight into their drinking patterns and clarify their associations with drinking. They may be surprised, even shocked, by how much they drink. For some, the drinking diary is the turning point that enables them to realize more clearly and forcefully their need to make changes, an opportunity to engage with that configuration of self, or set of configurations, that is carrying an urge towards reduced alcohol intake or abstinence. It helps them to engage with their feelings for change; seeing how much they spend, or the damaging effects, can stimulate their desire to change.

Some say the problematic drinker will not be honest. This is a myth. Counselling is not about extracting a confession. It is about being open with clients, letting them know that it can be a helpful process, even though it may be discomfiting. The only person a client will really deceive is themselves. In my experience, clients generally appreciate a counsellor's frankness. Comments such as: 'So you reckon you drink 40 units, well, I'm going to double that then,' are unhelpful, belittling, and disrespectful, but they do occur. The fact is, in my experience, that the problematic drinker is no more likely to lie than anyone else when talking about something painful and difficult to accept. Often the evasive client is experiencing a high level of shame, and is struggling to make what they are doing visible to another person, and to themselves. This can reflect a tremendous inner struggle between configurations. Clients may need time to trust the counsellor and to feel sufficiently comfortable in the relationship to begin to accept and make visible their inner drama.

The client, having begun to think about change, may also need to explore what gains and losses there might be. This is crucial. The losses could sabotage the attempts to change. These need to be identified and, when the client is ready to make changes, he or she will want to plan ways of ensuring that these factors do not obstruct them in achieving their goal. I have found that offering the idea of looking at the short- and long-term benefits and losses of change, or of continuing to drink at the current rate, can be helpful for some people at this stage. Again, though, stress is placed on the idea of offering it. The client's autonomy to choose his or her own way of making sense of choices is respected.

If it seems relevant, I might offer the idea of the client drawing a lifeline (Figure 4.2). At a point just ahead of the present there is a fork; one line continues straight on – representing continued drinking – while the other branches upwards – representing change, reduced drinking or abstinence, depending on what the client is seeking. Possibilities are then plotted against these two lines in a herring-bone style. This can help the client to gain a picture of his or her choice, of the effects of change. By projecting it on to paper, externalizing it, they can gain a clearer overview that can help them to make an informed choice. It often helps in bringing the client's reality into the therapeutic setting.

Having weighed up the pros and cons, not everyone will choose to change. It may be too frightening. Perhaps the person simply feels that life with heavy alcohol use is, for him

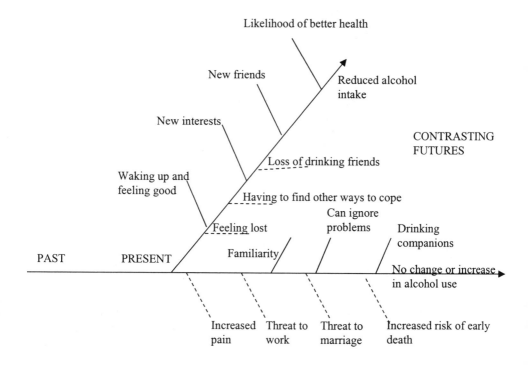

Figure 4.2 Example of a lifeline

or her, more satisfying than life without or with less. The very idea of changing the alcohol use may be actually unthinkable in his or her circumstances, which he or she feels powerless to change. There is therefore an exit point within the contemplation phase. Should the client take this route, it is helpful, as with the pre-contemplator, to convey that should they wish to revisit the topic of change, the door is open to this. I would hope to be authentic in this situation as well, conveying any concerns that I might have while respecting the client's right to choose.

Exiting from the contemplation phase does not mean that counselling should end. The client may wish to explore other areas of his or her life and it can be a powerful message to the client to accept this. A danger with alcohol counselling services is the excessive focus on alcohol use, as a result of which a decision by the client not to change could lead to a withdrawal of service. Yet a therapeutic relationship has been created and may be used so that other issues, more pressing for the client, can be addressed. This can then, given time, lead to the client making the decision to address their level and pattern of alcohol use.

Planning change

The client who recognizes a need to change will begin to enter a phase of planning. It may take a while to get to this point. The person-centred counsellor is not going to hurry a client into an early decision. The plan itself needs to be owned by the client. It is a collaborative process, an exploration together of what the client feels they can work towards. The goals that are agreed have to be realistic, otherwise the risk is that clients are set up to fail. It is far more encouraging for someone to aim for a gradual reduction and achieve it than to aim for a big reduction and be unable to reach the goal.

It is good to have a system of monitoring the amount being drunk. Here, the drinking diary can be useful as a way of targeting the reduction and keeping track of it. It is good to agree a clear start time so that the reduction is not always going to begin next week, which then somehow never happens. When it is always put off, clearly something is present that is strong enough to cause the client to hesitate. Perhaps the therapist has made an assumption regarding the client's readiness to change, or led them into a decision that they are not ready for. When the counsellor has a sense that this is happening, it is best voiced and explored. It is also an issue for supervision, particularly if it occurs often. It may indicate that the therapist is centred on their own agenda of promoting change, rather than on the client's process.

I find that the exploration of, and planning for, change has to involve my being authentic: genuine concerns are expressed, encouragement and support are offered. Readiness to face up to the reality of the situation becomes present in the relationship. The person behind the problematic drinking behaviour is being engaged with and is being allowed to flourish.

The risk of relapse can usefully be discussed at this stage. The process of looking at the benefits and losses will have highlighted some of the potential relapse triggers. They need to be explored and may require additional planning. The counsellor can offer the view that change is often a journey into the unknown, that people do not know how they will react or respond until they are making the change. The unexpected can happen, or things can be more difficult than anticipated. People can deny that they have a problem, this we know; they can also deny that there is any possibility of relapse because they do not want to think about it. The client's choice in this is respected; however, genuinely felt concern is also voiced.

It is not that relapse is a 'bad thing', but it can be avoided along with a lot of unnecessary difficulties that may arise as a result. If aspects of an individual's structure of self can be identified as having a strong link to problematic alcohol use, and they can be worked on in such a way that they become accepted and not feared, and reintegrated in such a way that they do not present in such a highly sensitive and reactive form, their impact as relapse triggers can be reduced. If relapse prevention can reduce the risk of relapse and the effects that can result (loss of job, break-up of a relationship, damage to health, suicide attempts, death) then I would argue that it has a place in a respectful, person-to-person helping relationship.

I often find that the client's willingness, or not, to plan for the possibility of relapse during this phase is a good indicator of whether congruence is truly present, or rather, the degree of incongruence. When clients avoid considering ways of minimizing the risk of relapse there is often an unwillingness to engage with a set of feelings linked to this possibility. Readiness to plan and to acknowledge these feelings openly indicates that the client is more realistic. Success is more likely. Either way, the therapeutic relationship will offer clients the unconditional warmth and acceptance that will encourage them to maintain contact should they relapse.

Action

The plan has been made and now comes the time to put it into operation. Support will be required; perhaps the person will want to ensure the family is supportive, maybe friends will be giving encouragement. The change is very likely to be not just about cutting back on the alcohol intake. People can lose a lot of time through drinking. When the drinking is reduced it is important to plan other satisfying activities and interests to replace it, otherwise a vacuum is created in the client's life with every risk that the old drinking pattern will be sucked back in.

Many heavy drinkers find they need a strongly flavoured drink. Anything less is not so satisfying. So if they are going to drink something non-alcoholic, it needs to have some bite to it, certainly to begin with. Clients say how things lose their appeal, 'I can't taste it, there's no pleasure in it'. It is not that there is a lack of flavour, but that their taste sensitivity has altered. It often comes back in time, however, if the person persists in drinking less highly flavoured drinks.

Action may involve major changes of routine. This can be a time of great stress, which in itself could be one of the factors triggering the client to drink. In what other ways can stress be handled? Can it be avoided? Too much change can be unsettling and overwhelming. It comes back to being realistic. Small, sustainable steps are often easier to handle. Also, who knows about the planned change? Pressure can be unbearable from people who do not appreciate that someone is trying to change a drinking habit. Generally, the more open the client is about it, the greater the chance of success. Having someone pressuring them with 'just have the one, it won't hurt you' without having any planned response can be a serious problem. It is often difficult for someone to tell people that they are planning to cut back or stop, particularly if friends or family members are themselves heavy drinkers. However, this is important. Many heavy drinkers soon discover who their true friends are, and who the saboteurs are, who themselves feel threatened by the idea of one of their number acknowledging the need to change.

Maintenance and exit

The client has initiated change; now comes a lengthy phase of maintaining that change. Support systems will have been planned to minimize the risk of relapse. These need to be maintained. People often think, when they have made their change, that that is it, and are tempted to go it alone. 'Well, I've cut back, I'm feeling better, no need to see you now, is there?' It is generally much better to maintain contact and support. It is early days, things can happen to catch people out. It can be a very uncertain time and review and forward planning on a regular basis can be extremely helpful. The client who wants to move on too quickly may again be denying feelings of concern, may be acting out of incongruence. Yet they may be right, they may have sufficiently changed within themselves to sustain the outer change of the drinking habit. The more congruence within the relationship, the greater the likelihood that the client will be able to acknowledge the truth of what is present, and the risk of breaking away from support too soon is minimized.

It is also likely that, as time goes by, frequency of contact, or even the length of sessions, will be reduced. When the client's primary focus is on reducing the alcohol intake, I have found that there comes a point when the client feels ready for half-hourly sessions every couple of weeks, or maybe, in time, monthly sessions. This can be helpful and I think counsellors can be too rigid over frequency and length of counselling contact. Some clients find an occasional appointment is enough for them, providing a kind of safety net as they spend more and more time 'going it alone'. Yet this has to be when the time is right, and the person-centred counsellor trusts the client to be the best judge of that. Sessions may also become increasingly conversational, as the client moves on. Here I find it useful to talk this through with the client, and in supervision, to maintain clarity on the way the counselling relationship is developing and what the client's needs are.

The client is likely to be faced with people who do not understand the difficulty of establishing a change of drinking habit. 'What do you mean, you had a drink, you told me you were stopping. You're just not taking this seriously, are you?' Or the person who insists on asking them, constantly, 'Have you been drinking?' or worse still, whenever something goes wrong, 'I knew it, you've been drinking again. I knew you couldn't change'. People who only ever ask about the alcohol use, or always begin with the same question (particularly with a tone of judgement and condemnation) – 'How much are you drinking?' – can be irritating and stress-generating, offering little respect for the person who is doing his best. As one client put it:

It just knocks you back. All that you have achieved gets wiped out. You want a bit of encouragement and someone saying 'well done', or appreciating the struggle you have had. All you get is 'How much are you drinking then?' voiced with an air of expectation that you haven't changed or tried to change.

Yet, at the same time, the person who is stressed by someone else's drinking is going to find it hard not to react or to suspect alcohol has been used on occasions. It is often quite a struggle to rebuild trust. Others can have unrealistic expectations as well. The attitudes and behaviour of other family members powerfully influence sustainable change. Couple or family therapy can enable those most closely involved to appreciate their roles in supporting the drinker in maintaining change, and help to keep lines of communication open.

For many people who have maintained their change for a few months, it will have become established. They have left the cycle of change. Perhaps they have brought their alcohol intake down to within safe drinking limits and are happy to stay with that. Fine. Maybe they have achieved abstinence. It is important that they know where to go if they need support. People exit from maintenance when they have moved on within themselves from a preoccupation with alcohol, when they are effectively getting on with their lives. They are maintaining their change, it is no longer a routine struggle.

Relapse

Relapse happens, and it is important to try to help the person unravel it and make sense of it, yet at the same time to enable them to feel supported and allowed to say or simply feel what is present for them. The person who genuinely seeks to cut back on their drinking, who has carefully planned how they are going to do it, does not tend to relapse with intent. It is often the result of something unexpected and unplanned, perhaps the return of an old drinking friend who has been away, or a circumstance that rekindles an old and painful memory.

Another type of relapse is when the alcohol has clearly been used as a coping mechanism for feelings that have not been resolved. The reduced alcohol use, or abstinence, means that the anaesthetic effect is reduced as well, and painful or difficult feelings can break through and overwhelm people, drawing them back into alcohol use or heavier alcohol use. It may be that a previously unrecognized 'alcohol using' configuration of self has emerged, or developed. Hence the need, so often, to work on underlying feelings, and to adopt an holistic perspective and way of working. Changing a drinking pattern is not the end of the story. There are often many other threads and connections to the drinking; sustainable change generally requires these to be included, and engaged with, within the therapeutic process.

Part of the plan may have been an agreement that the counsellor will initiate contact with the client if it seems that relapse has occurred. While a person has the right to choose to return to an old drinking pattern, this choice may be alcohol-affected, and not what the person really wants, but they can feel powerless to stop given the alcohol's effect on motivation and mood. The plan could include an agreement that a relative, the GP or a social worker, for instance, will contact the counsellor, or that the counsellor will phone immediately if the client does not attend a session. What is important is early contact to give the client the chance of not returning to the old drinking pattern. It may only be a lapse but the danger is that it can become a relapse.

This may not be possible and the client may relapse heavily, break contact and return to the old drinking problem. He or she may stop seeking change and in effect return to being a pre-contemplator. One of the challenges that I find in working with clients with alcohol problems is that contact can be broken suddenly, with a developing or developed person-to-person relationship left in the air. Supervision is vital in helping me to come to terms with this. I am often left with feelings of sadness, wondering whether our sessions should have been different in some way, or whether maybe I missed something. While I accept that the client has autonomy, I also appreciate the mood-altering impact of heavy alcohol use, and so a sudden loss of contact due to a heavy relapse will often fill me with feelings of compassion and concern, and with a certain sense of helplessness when a letter or phone message is not replied to.

However, the client who relapses may choose to remain in touch with their earlier motivation and move back into contemplation, rethink their action plan and redevise it in the light of their relapse experience.

Person-centred approach to the model of change

We can view the cycle of change specifically from the perspective of the person-centred approach and theory. It would be tempting to try to relate congruence and incongruence directly to the stages of change; however, I do not believe this is possible or helpful. Both may be present throughout the cycle. Consider the person contemplating change. It could be congruent sensitivity to alcohol-induced discomfort that triggers the urge to change; or it could be psychological discomfort stemming from incongruence that the alcohol no longer anaesthetizes. For the person in relapse, again it could be congruence that has been the trigger, a congruent experience of an overwhelmingly painful situation; or incongruence as a difficult situation may have been magnified and exacerbated a poor self-concept born out of negative conditioning to unmanageable levels.

I believe the person-centred approach can be accommodated within the framework of the cycle of change. The model does not say that you must do this or that at particular stages, rather it indicates what is more likely to be relevant and helpful to the client. While it creates a framework for what is likely to occur, what is actually taking place will be centred on the client themselves. They may well be experiencing ambivalence, unsure as to whether they want to change or not. The person-centred approach requires the client not to be directed into a particular action or way of thinking, but allowed to explore what is present for them, the counsellor accepting and seeking to communicate back to the client their understanding of what is being said and experienced. The client is thereby enabled to engage with their own thoughts and feelings, and to reach their own conclusions based on a realistic appraisal of their situation and increasing self-awareness.

When the counsellor has empathic rapport with the inner world of the client, their motivations, their hopes, their fears, their goals, then they are with them as a companion. Trust in the actualizing tendency, along with the presence of the core conditions within the relationship, encourages the clients to seek a 'growthful' and realistic response to their situation. They will begin to weigh up the positive and negative features of changing their drinking pattern for themselves. The counsellor's empathy and warm acceptance encourages their exploration to become more open. Previously unrecognized feelings may emerge into awareness, and into the room; fresh perspectives on the situation will come to mind; the urge to achieve a more fulfilling lifestyle can become powerfully present.

The communication by the therapist, and the experience by the client, of the core conditions is likely to enable the client to feel able to voice any concerns he or she may have about relapse, or the person-centred counsellor will have genuinely sensed their presence and acted on an urge to voice them himself. So the need to talk about relapse will naturally come about. Ensuring that the planning is realistic will be important to the clients. They will want to achieve their goal and will not want to feel coerced into striving to achieve too great a reduction. Again, empathic sensitivity in the counsellor will be the factor that ensures that this concern is sensed, and the presence of congruence that such concern will be voiced by the counsellor. Warmth or unconditional positive regard experienced by the client will encourage a sense of acceptance that will enable them to feel their concerns are legitimized.

At the same time, the counsellor's own authenticity and transparency will help ensure that, when they experience concerns about something that the client is suggesting, these will be voiced in a warm and supportive manner. Of course, the increasingly empowered client may well insist on doing it their way and this may fly in the face of all that the counsellor believes would be helpful. I have seen this lead to positive outcomes in terms of the client achieving their goal, much to my surprise, particularly when clients have cut back dramatically after a first contact and have managed to maintain that reduced level of drinking. Yet for others, it does not work out; this may lead them to return to explore what went wrong, or they may break contact.

There is an element of truth in the idea that 'the client is going to do what the client is going to do'. As a counsellor, I may express my congruently held feelings of concern, but the client will make his or her own choices. They will approach change with their own style. This may be genuinely their own. Alternatively, they may be feeling pressured. For instance, they may be a person who would benefit from a gradual step-by-step, methodical approach to change, but their family style may be knee-jerk reaction without forward planning, which may lead to pressure on the person to reduce quickly or just stop without thought of the consequences. Some may undertake change in a manner that is symptomatic of past conditioning, such as the person who, at an early age, while wanting and needing support and prizing from significant others, received little or none and so had to develop an independent streak. They now find it hard to accept help later in life; they may decide to do it their own way, not wanting further support, suggestions or time to explore with a counsellor.

The great challenge to the person-centred counsellor working within the cycle of change framework is that of the simplicity of being with the client without having an agenda, or goals, that the client 'should' achieve. The cycle of change was designed in the context of changing behaviour as a goal. Yet the person-centred counsellor is more concerned with how he or she is in relationship with the client, trusting that 'growthful' change will occur as a product of that relationship, but not carrying an attitude of 'doing person-centred' in order to promote growth. It cannot be too strongly emphasized that the person-centred approach is a way of being with the client, not a technique to be applied to effect a particular outcome.

I am even unsure whether 'growth' is the right word; it seems to me that I am helping people to generate more satisfying experiences, both within themselves and through the relationships that they develop, that proceed out of a self-structure less affected by conditions of worth. The form these experiences will take will vary from individual to individual. I am hopeful that this offers to the client a greater measure of the 'fuller functionality' that Rogers refers to.

Raising the issue of alcohol

With the cycle of change in mind, issues arise when working with a person whose drinking is problematic yet who has not acknowledged this. The main emphasis here is on when, whether and how the issue of alcohol use can be raised within the person-centred approach. There are certain key points to bear in mind:

- The issue is being raised as a legitimate concern, based on something that has become evident either through the client's behaviour, or because of something they have disclosed.

- The concern is genuine and not an 'empty technique' designed to make an impact.

- Any comments, suggestions and/or advice offered are clear and based on reliable information.

In my experience it is important to be firm and clear without straying into being judgemental. It is helpful for the counsellor to build a relationship with the client before making any comment about alcohol intake, bearing in mind the need to be congruent.

There is also the matter of who raises the issue of a person's alcohol intake in a counselling setting. As an alcohol counsellor I am more likely to respond to an indicated high alcohol intake than when I am working as a general counsellor. I have a different remit. Yet there have been times when it has been appropriate to voice my concern in general counselling, simply because that is what I am feeling in response to what has been disclosed to me. It is a voicing of concern, a congruent expression from a fellow human being. The client, however, will be free to take it up, or not. That is their choice, and they must surely be left free with this.

In medical settings there are many health professionals who have a clear remit to raise the issue of problematic drinking, or act on a belief that alcohol use is causing problems. Counsellors work in these settings as part of multi-disciplinary teams. At what point might a counsellor raise the issue of alcohol use with the client and/or with a medical practitioner? Consider a client who is disclosing a range of health problems that could be alcohol-related and probably require urgent medical intervention, or one whose mood is low with a suspected drinking relapse that in the past led to suicidal intent. It seems to me that in both these instances the counsellor has a legitimate reason to express genuinely held feelings of concern to the client, and in some circumstances to their GP.

Has the confidentiality contract agreed with the client defined explicit limitations of confidentiality? Working in medical settings within multi-disciplinary teams can alter the role of the counsellor, and clarity on confidentiality and boundaries is essential. Counsellors working in medical settings will come across clients with alcohol problems, and those using other substances as well as mood-altering prescribed medications. There is a need to know when to refer on for medical intervention.

In private practice, at what point might a counsellor voice experienced concerns over a client's drinking? When the client:

- arrives intoxicated?

- discloses that his or her level of drinking is well above a safe drinking level?

- discloses behaviour associated with drinking that harms others or themselves?

- reveals suicidal thoughts during heavy binge-drinking?

○ cancels and it is clear from the background noise that
they are in a pub?

Counsellors are fundamentally health-care professionals; they
may be in a position to raise concern over possible problematic
alcohol use, and will need to be clear as to when they would
decide to do this. It could be after developing a trusting relationship with the client, but there may be occasions when the
issue is too pressing to be delayed, for instance, if the personal
safety of the client, the counsellor, or others is in question; or in
the case of inability to sustain a reasonable level of psychological contact, for instance if the client is not able to hear the
voiced concerns of the therapist because of suspected high
levels of intoxication or withdrawal symptoms.

In workplace settings or Employee Assistance Programmes,
the counsellor has to be clear on their remit regarding clients'
alcohol use at work, particularly when an employee's contract
prohibits them from working while under the influence of
alcohol, or when a client's alcohol use puts their own, or
another's, life at risk. Raising the issue of alcohol use then has
added significance. The counsellor needs to know their role,
the limits to confidentiality, and to whom they should disclose
concerns within an employing organization. It is important for
these to be made clear to the client at first contact.

The intoxicated client

There remains the issue of whether to see the alcohol-affected
client. The client who has had a drink could be a pre-contemplator, a contemplator, someone maintaining a reduced
alcohol intake, or a person in relapse. One can take the view
that to see someone for counselling while they are
alcohol-affected is to collude and legitimize what they are
doing and to encourage them. Yet refusing to see them could

be experienced as a rejection or a punishment, feeding into and exacerbating low self-worth.

Boundaries are needed, yet, on first contact, none have been set. The counsellor may choose congruently to confront the client who arrives under the influence yet is denying it as a problem. If they want to be seen, and presumably that is why they are there, the alcohol use is a problem because it is a barrier to them gaining what they want. The client may say that although it is a problem to the counsellor, it is not to them. The client is then confronted with the need to take into account the counsellor's feelings, needs and boundaries, and to take responsibility for the choice to drink before a session in the light of this.

When a counsellor has a policy of no alcohol before a session, I think they should at least be clear in their own mind as to why, and this can usefully be conveyed to the client. It can be made clear that it is not a matter of personal rejection, but one of belief that therapeutic work requires the client to be alcohol-free. Or it could be an issue of personal safety, which is a legitimate reason for not seeing particular clients. Yet it may be that the counsellor is discriminating against the drinker. It is a topic to think through and to process so that the counsellor can be quite clear in their own heart and mind their reasons for seeing, or not seeing, clients who are alcohol-affected. Also, what about the client who has no alcohol problem, but had half a pint of lager or a gin and tonic prior to the session because they arrived early and a pub was nearby? Will they be treated in the same way as the person with an alcohol problem who had the same amount to drink?

It is unrealistic to expect a client to be alcohol-free on the day of the appointment when they are a truly dependent drinker who simply needs a drink first thing in the morning to take away the shakes, or a psychologically dependent person who needs that drink to get out of the house. If your policy is not to see clients in that condition, referral on to a specialist alcohol service is necessary, and can usefully be offered in a supportive and understanding manner.

Person-centred counselling is very much a relational process that is both interpersonal and intrapersonal between and within the client and the therapist. It requires the presence of 'psychological contact' between client and therapist. Can the counsellor be in psychological contact with an intoxicated or alcohol-affected client? Yes, they can. In these circumstances, the presence of the client-centred counsellor alone can be enough for psychological contact to be achieved by maintaining a consistent and committed presence. Feedback from my clients has shown that they can be really appreciative of being seen when drunk, that for some it made them think about how badly affected they were and how necessary it was seriously to do something about their level of alcohol use. Turning away such a client, particularly without adequate explanation, risks feeding their low self-worth, affirming a sense of deserving constant rejection. They may never come back. An opportunity for change is lost.

I have sat with clients whose alcohol use has brought high levels of distress that are present in the session and I have sought to hold contact with the person before me. My instinct tells me so often in these situations that behind the alcohol-induced behaviour there is a person who is hurting, and probably hurting a great deal; a person who is frightened, who knows they are not coping and who is feeling very alone. The client-centred counsellor is there with them, reaching out to that person. The genuine attempt to enter into the relationship is a powerful intervention and is often appreciated by the client. It can be a challenge to a client's sense 'of being unlovable', or 'of only deserving rejection', offering them opportunity to risk redefining their self-concept a little.

Scenario 1

> *This is the second session. At the first, the counsellor was not sure whether Diane had been drinking; she had mentioned that she worked in a pub and the counsellor had assumed that the smell of alcohol probably came from her clothes. However, at this second session there is alcohol on her breath and she was a little wobbly when she came through the door.*

In the session the counsellor has thoughts going through their head concerning their belief that Diane has been drinking, perhaps heavily, prior to the session. Does the counsellor immediately make explicit these thoughts by voicing them? Do they hold back to see if the client makes some reference to it? It may not be a problem to the client, but it could be to the counsellor.

The person-centred counsellor will want to trust their empathic understanding of Diane's world, while at the same time holding to their own authenticity. Transparency is called for. It may be that the issue is sitting with the counsellor and obstructing the relationship. In such a case it needs voicing, but sensitively. The client has made the commitment of coming to the sessions and it is possible that she needed that drink to give herself confidence to get there. Perhaps Diane has gained something from the last session and a therapeutic relationship is developing that is helping her to trust the counsellor. The situation, if not handled sensitively, could leave her feeling rejected and she may never come back. Much will depend on the development of the relationship with the client. The counsellor may voice what he or she is feeling: 'I am sitting here with a strong sense that maybe alcohol is a factor and it leaves me concerned for your safety', or 'I am sensing that we are not communicating well, and I am wondering if alcohol use is linked to this'.

Whether the counsellor decides to raise the matter, or not, it is an issue for supervision. There is a need to explore why a particular decision was taken within the therapeutic setting. Was it a genuinely transparent and empathic response to the client rather than one clouded by issues within the counsellor? Diane's reaction may be one of total denial. The counsellor may find it valuable to hold in his mind or reflect on the differing experiences: 'You sound really clear that you have not been drinking while I am very aware of the smell of alcohol since you walked in'.

Strong denial, when it is clear the client is alcohol-affected, can indicate various experiences within the client: deep shame, unwillingness to risk judgement, a configuration in which alcohol use is denied as a matter of course, or the actual awareness of the drinking having been split off from consciousness. In the latter case, the client could be in the 'dissociative state' mentioned earlier (Warner 1991, 1998).

If the awareness of the alcohol use is a passing one that does not hold the counsellor's attention, then the person-centred counsellor is likely to let it go. It is the client's therapeutic hour. It is their right, and the counsellor's role, to ensure that the focus is on the client's chosen area of emphasis and not the counsellor's.

Scenario 2

> *This is the first session with Andy and it is 9am. The counsellor has not detected the smell of alcohol, but the client is very shaky. He is clearly highly anxious and finding it hard to concentrate and engage with the counsellor.*

The counsellor could be faced here with someone who is simply very anxious or has a medical condition, or with a dependent drinker who has not had a drink this morning but needs one to settle himself down. If it is the latter, Andy has perhaps managed to hold back because he wants to be dry for the session; maybe he feels ashamed and does not want the counsellor to know; maybe he really wants the session to help him and he feels a drink would have got in the way. What does the counsellor do?

I would highlight my awareness of how shaky Andy is, how anxious he seems to be. It is best not to jump to conclusions over alcohol use. He may have a neurological problem producing shaking which, because he finds this embarrassing, creates high anxiety. I would check out with Andy the background to the shakiness out of genuine concern and with warmth for him.

> *Counsellor:* I am so aware of your shaking and it is leaving me concerned for your well-being. I am wondering if what you are experiencing now is normal or unusual?
>
> *Andy:* Most mornings. It's been like this the last few weeks. I don't know why.
>
> *Counsellor:* Mhm, you don't know why.
>
> *Andy:* (*long silence*) Life's been more stressful.

However, I may still be left with a strong sense of the shakiness being alcohol-related and then comes the decision as to whether to voice this or not. It really does come down to how I am experiencing being with Andy in the moment. What impact is he having on me? The shaking is real. My concern is genuine and so I might voice the possibility of alcohol use to try to clarify the situation. 'It's not unusual for people to shake in the mornings when they are drinking heavily': this leaves an opening for Andy to respond.

When alcohol use is denied, do not push it. Accept the client's perspective. Perhaps there is no alcohol problem, or, if there is, maybe as the relationship develops, Andy will be more able to risk making it more visible and engaging with it in the session. At this initial session Andy may have more pressing issues to disclose and explore and will not want the counsellor to direct him into a particular area of his life that he does not want to talk about. It may be that what Andy wants is 'someone to hear how I am feeling, not go on about what I am doing'. Later on in the therapeutic relationship, when confidence is established, he may feel able to disclose areas that are more difficult to voice.

Scenario 3

> *The counsellor has seen Pat for 12 sessions over the past 6 months. It has been a very engaging therapeutic relationship, she has been working at resolving her grief following the death of her husband earlier in the year. Much progress has been made. Alcohol has not featured as an issue. She has been developing a new lifestyle. However, today Pat has been drinking, the counsellor is sure of it, though Pat has not mentioned it. She is simply extremely upset and full of grief for her husband.*

The relationship has developed between Pat and the counsellor to a point at which there is mutual trust and she is able to use the time to share her grief. This is the issue she is in the room with. Later in the session may come the moment to understand what has triggered her current level of distress and how alcohol has been drawn into the picture, but now she needs space, she needs a companion in her grief, she needs to feel the counsellor's presence as a human being with her in her struggle.

Suddenly introducing the topic of alcohol will not be appropriate. It will invade her world, being an intrusion into what she is wanting to convey. As a person-centred counsellor I will trust her to find her own way through her grief. If the topic of alcohol is raised by a counsellor in these situations, it could be a defence against the client's feelings of grief and distress that induce discomfort in the therapist. It can distract the focus that the client has brought which is her grief. Feelings towards her alcohol use may not be the ones uppermost in her 'here and now' experience. They may become so as she feels heard and supported in her grief.

Pat may not mention alcohol. So how does the counsellor then respond? There is nothing verbal to respond to. The counsellor may leave it, or offer her the opportunity to share anything else that is on her mind. From the client's perspective, the alcohol use in this instance has probably been a coping mechanism, a support, and is probably not seen in any way as a problem. As a person-centred counsellor I would respect this viewpoint and it is unlikely that I would raise the issue unless it continues to nag at me. Then my own need to maintain transparency would urge me to mention the alcohol. I place great faith in attending to nagging elements that will not go away, and they generally have relevance when they are voiced, often having a releasing effect, and allowing the client to touch into something important. In this instance, with a relationship that is well established, a one-word question can be powerful if voiced with respect and warmth by the counsellor: 'Alcohol?'

Final comments

I have come across situations in which people have expressed to a health-care professional that they wished the subject of alcohol had been brought up by the professional earlier. They recognize that, while they would have felt angry and ashamed at the time, and might have tried to deny it (or might not), it would have helped them to have had that other person draw attention to it. This would have offered them an opportunity to address the issue, and thereby possibly helped to avoid things getting a lot worse before they began to get better.

In raising the issue of alcohol use, the communication of the core conditions as the basis for the therapeutic relationship between client and counsellor is a crucial factor. The counsellor is seeking to be transparent, to be open to the client's concerns and empathic sensitivity, and to communicate this in a way that is warm, non-judgemental and sensitive to the client's inner world. When the persistent feeling is present that alcohol is a factor, it is highly likely that voicing it will be helpful.

Key points

- People pass through stages of change.
- Where the person is within the cycle of change governs the kind of responses that will be helpful.
- Relapse is often a part of the process of establishing sustainable change.
- Clarity of the counsellor's remit is needed when working in different settings.
- Raising the issue of unvoiced alcohol use is generally helpful when the counsellor has a strong and persistent sense that it is a factor.
- Some people cannot attend for counselling without having had alcohol on the day.
- It is helpful to know who the local specialist alcohol counselling services are, in case it is necessary for a client to be referred on to them.

CHAPTER 5

From Pre-Contemplation to Taking Action

When congruent concern over alcohol use is brought up within the counselling relationship, some clients will deny catagorically that alcohol use is a problem. They may truly not have a problem, or they may have a problem and be unable to acknowledge it, even though they present as being intoxicated and there is a clear smell of alcohol. Many people who drink problematically, particularly at the dependent end of the spectrum, have a tendency to deny it to their family, to a counsellor, and even to themselves.

They may be fearful of what might happen, of what they might have to do, of who else might get to know. Nobody likes to admit to being unable to control something in their lives. We like to feel on top of things and in charge of our actions and choices. It is not uncommon for dependent drinkers to hide bottles and cans, even when they live alone. This is often labelled as being intentionally devious. In some cases this is true, in others the drinker is deeply ashamed and unable or unwilling to face up to what they are doing.

The fear of having alcohol taken away can stop people acknowledging their problematic drinking. Being open about it might mean having to face the feelings that they know would surface if they could not drink regularly. This can be very scary. These may be the very emotions they have been using the alcohol to suppress for a long time, or the very intense feelings that can arise in withdrawal.

The person-centred counsellor's response is to be empathic to the client's world and to express what they observe and experience, in a way that will endeavour to reach beyond the alcohol dependence to the, at times, very frightened person behind. At the extreme end of the problematic drinking continuum are those who are almost 'professional drinkers' – it is their identity and their whole daily routine. They have no thoughts whatsoever of stopping. What can be done to help these people?

Harm minimization

Realism means taking a harm minimization perspective – an approach used widely in working with drug and alcohol users. This means, first of all, taking the pragmatic view that some clients are going to choose to drink problematically and that the counselling interaction can be a means of helping to ensure that they do as little damage to themselves and others as possible. Harm minimization can be regarded as a message to avoid problems when drinking (Plant *et al.* 1997). In taking this approach, the counsellor is also sending the client another message that is crucially important – that they care and that to them the client has worth. The client's experience of the counsellor's unconditional positive regard has enormous therapeutic value. It challenges a self-concept that may have been shaped largely through conditioned responses, put-downs, rejections and losses. When this is coupled with the counsellor's authenticity and endeavour to communicate empathy, an opportunity for change is offered.

A harm minimization approach might include the following considerations:

- What is the client's accommodation situation? Contact with the local housing department might be encouraged. Is the client sleeping rough? If so, could they be helped to obtain accommodation in a hostel or 'wet house' (supported residential accommodation where alcohol use is allowed)? Do they know whom they might contact about this?

- Is the client not eating because their money goes on alcohol? Could they be encouraged to go to any local community care services providing hot food?

- Have they a GP? They might be encouraged to register and to be given a health check. Have they had tests for liver damage? If not, local alcohol agencies can often arrange these.

- Are they drinking dependently and at risk of withdrawal fits and therefore in need of hospitalization or medication in order to reduce? If so, referral for assessment for detoxification will be appropriate. The harm minimization perspective views a detoxification, even if the person returns to drinking, as a positive achievement.

- Are there financial problems affecting the drinker or his/her family? Encouragement to contact local agencies offering advice can be offered.

- What effect is the drinker having on the family? Are there other support services involved, or that should be called in? Are the children safe? Drinking heavily does not automatically bring parenting skills into question, but the counsellor may be sufficiently concerned to want to involve social services; has this been catered for explicitly within the counselling contract and boundaries to confidentiality?

- ∘ There may be mental health issues that need addressing, either the effect of alcohol use, or problems being self-medicated through the alcohol use: depression, anxiety states, schizophrenia, paranoia, suicidal intent. Is a mental health referral required? In extreme cases, is concern about the physical or mental well-being of the client enough to call an ambulance there and then?

- ∘ Is the client drinking neat spirits? A move towards either diluting or switching some of the alcohol intake to lower strength drinks might be appropriate. If the client is drinking strong lager, beer or cider, perhaps they might switch to some of lower strength, reducing the concentration of alcohol.

- ∘ Are information leaflets available to pass on to the client? They must be appropriate, offering clear and reliable information presented non-judgementally and in a manner sensitive to the drinker's world of experience.

- ∘ If the client is a relative of a problematic drinker, they may need to know whom to contact for advice, information and support.

Some of these may seem to be beyond the remit of a counsellor. Or are they? They are not outside the naturally human response towards another person; they demonstrate that someone cares which itself is a powerful therapeutic response. I would argue that a harm minimization response can be an expression of unconditional positive regard for the client.

If the counsellor can remain with the client during the drinking phase, offering consistency, authenticity and unconditional positive regard, there is a chance of change. The client may only maintain contact for a short while, but a seed is sown. Very often it makes sufficient impression for the client to return at a later date when they have moved on within themselves. Perhaps they are then more prepared to consider or accept their need to change (moving into contemplation); they may be drawn back by a sense that the therapeutic relationship is what they need, without any clear understanding of where they wish it to take them. At some level they are aware of the warmth and acceptance of the earlier relationship and it feels a safe place to return to, in order to face up to the risky business of change.

What moves people to change?

The urge to change is generally driven by a mix of not wanting to continue with something that is uncomfortable and/or wanting to achieve a greater sense of well-being. What is crucial is that the problematic drinker themselves experiences this urge. 'I woke up one morning, the sun was shining and I asked myself, "What am I doing?" I knew I had to change.' 'I found myself with someone whom I'd met the previous night. I didn't know who he was. I'd been drunk. I hadn't put myself at this much risk before.' These kinds of experience can drive people into contemplating change.

Sometimes, it can be the impact of others that encourages the urge to change. 'It was the GP, she told me in no uncertain terms what the risks were if I carried on.' 'When my family gave me an ultimatum – the whole family – I realized something was seriously wrong. Fortunately, they were also understanding and supportive and helped me as I made my decision to stop drinking.'

It may be an alcohol-related experience or event which is significant: a drink-driving offence; seeing a friend in a coma after overdosing following a heavy drinking session; severe stomach pain; job loss. 'At first I went downhill and drank more heavily. A long talk with a friend who had overcome problems with alcohol helped me to think about the future again; I realized I had a problem.' It could even be a familiar setting, but now seen in a fresh light. 'I was lying on the sofa at home as I did most days, with a bottle, and I suddenly found myself thinking, 'Is this really much different from lying on a park bench?' I guess I looked over an edge and didn't like what I saw. It made me think about where I was heading.'

Most of these experiences could have led to continued drinking to cope with the discomfort of the insight. The dividing line between an experience triggering change, and triggering renewed alcohol use, is extremely fine. It is not simply the event which is important, but also the way the person experiences and interprets it, and then chooses to respond. The risk is that old patterns of reaction may assert themselves.

At first, the problematic drinker will be unsure: they are beginning to contemplate something very different for themselves, which can engender great anxiety and bring to the surface negative thoughts and feelings towards themselves, and often great self-doubt. Yet coupled with this is the urge to grow out of their current situation, to discover something more fulfilling. Some aspect of their nature is fighting back, seeking growth towards a more satisfying way of being. AA looks at it in a slightly different way: 'becoming sick and tired of being sick and tired' is a phrase I have heard many people use. It is a vulnerable time and yet can be a period when the person experiences great inner strength as well. The companionship of a counsellor, or others who can offer support and encouragement, is often crucially important to enable the person to maintain, at their own pace, their momentum of change. Offering psychological contact and the communication of the core conditions provides the growth-enhancing climate within which the seeds of new possibilities can flourish.

Time to contemplate

People can spend a long time contemplating change, possibly a whole lifetime. We have only to think of ourselves and how long we may have deliberated over something: when to decorate the front room, whether to end a relationship, what to do about all the rubbish in the loft, whether to join the gym. Of course, not everyone takes a long time, decisions can also be taken and acted on very quickly.

Similarly, the problematic drinker may need a long time to come to a decision. Changing an established drinking pattern will mean accepting the loss of some of or all the alcohol and is likely to involve many other radical changes. Time is needed to explore as many facets as possible of the considered change. Significant life-changes are being contemplated; there are niggling doubts, fears and anxieties; the counsellor is likely to spend a lot of time with the contemplating client. The more informed the client is, the more considered and owned will be their decision, and the greater the chance that conditioned urges to drink will be unravelled and new behaviour patterns planned and established. This will make successful and sustainable change, if chosen, much more likely.

We will consider some scenarios and explore what can be useful to clients at this stage.

Scenario 4

> *Jane has been attending counselling for three months. She self-referred because of stress due to work problems and pressure. She commutes and works long hours. She has generated a number of useful strategies to cope, including making more space for herself and being more assertive in maintaining her boundaries. From the counsellor's perspective, they seem to have helped. During the course of the current session she discloses that she had been reading a leaflet passed round at work that indicated 'safe*

drinking' limits. Jane has never spoken to the counsellor about her drinking, but she now talks about her concern at the bottle of wine, and sometimes a little more, she drinks each night to help her relax, and she expresses some anger towards the leaflet. She is unsure as to whether she has a problem, or what to do.

Jane is expressing a number of feelings: anger at seemingly being told what is good for her, concern in case she is doing herself damage and/or anxiety over the idea of changing what has become an established routine.

She will need time to engage with and clarify her various reactions. She may deny that she has a problem, yet the fact that she is there talking about it indicates that she is uneasy. Her ability to make her own choice is to be respected. Applying the person-centred approach involves the counsellor seeking an empathic understanding of the client's internal frame of reference and communicating that understanding, trusting the process of staying in touch with Jane's world. Jane will clarify her own feelings, will sense more accurately her comforts and discomforts, and will begin to formulate for herself what her priorities are, leaving her with the autonomy to make her own choice as to whether to cut back, or continue. She has the facts to base her decision on – the leaflet. The counsellor supports her and enables her to find a way of resolving her discomfort in a manner that is satisfying. The important thing is to avoid telling Jane whether or not she has a problem, or pushing her towards thinking about change.

How Jane reacts will indicate where she is in the cycle of change. She may drop the subject and move on to another, reflecting a decision not to change. However, she may continue wrestling with her conflicting feelings for the rest of this session and beyond. If she decides to reduce her drinking, her anxiety is likely to be focused on losing part of her daily routine. One thing to be careful of is not to categorize too quickly. Jane is the one who puts herself at a stage of change, not the counsellor. The counsellor is using the cycle to define which responses are likely to be helpful.

If she is thinking about change, the idea of the drinking diary could be offered to Jane to help her gain insight into the associations she has with drinking and to enhance her awareness of the choices she is making. Knowing the strength of the wine and how to work out units might help her to gain further clarity. If she is intimating feelings of wanting to change, she may wish to focus on the pros and cons of changing or not changing.

Jane may prefer to talk through and process the feelings that are present for her in the 'here and now' of the therapeutic relationship. She may want to explore what alcohol means to her, what her relationship is with that daily bottle of wine. How important is it to her? When she thinks of the evening ahead, what does she look forward to? How does it leave her feeling later in the evening? What does the bottle of wine give her that is so important that it has provoked an angry reaction? Is it being used to reduce stress, to wind down before going to sleep? Alcohol can help people sleep, but it is not quality sleep and in fact prolonged alcohol use can encourage insomnia.

Scenario 5

> George has come for his second counselling session. He discloses that the day after his first session he was stopped when driving and breathalysed – he was found to be twice over the limit. He is going to be prosecuted. He does not know what to do about his drinking. It had never seemed a problem until now. He does not drink every day, but gets through half a bottle of whisky maybe three or four times a week, and some wine with meals on occasions. He is at home all day, bored and lonely. Ever since he retired he has felt

low. His partner is still working and is not around during the daytime. He is confused by what has happened.

This scenario contains typical elements that a client may bring to a session. George has a range of feelings and thoughts linked to the drink-driving. He is left wondering whether he has a problem with his drinking. He knows he should not have driven under the influence of alcohol, but is his actual drinking a problem beyond this? There is an element of the alcohol filling time. Loneliness and isolation are common connections with alcohol use. George's drinking may seem to him to be a solution more than a problem. Also, he has undergone a loss – of his job through retirement. His work has been his life and now he is feeling empty, struggling to create a new routine of living, or rather he has created a new routine that is largely alcohol-centred. Maybe he has not made many friends outside work, and so the drink becomes an attractive 'friend' to him now. Or he has a habit of using alcohol in times of loss.

George is going to need time and freedom to explore and make sense of the many feelings, thoughts and experiences that have impacted on him over a short space of time. It may be that since the breathalyser he has stopped drinking; this is a common reaction. So while there is part of him struggling with whether he has a problem and what he should do, another part has cut in and urged him to stop. He may need to explore whether he really wants to remain abstinent and, if so, he is likely to need to plan how. Or he may see it as a knee-jerk reaction, a short-term response, and have every intention of having a drink again in the future, but being more mindful of drinking and driving.

George may place emphasis on his confusion. It is very likely that he will swing back and forth between thinking about how to cope with the week ahead, and how he is feeling in the present moment. There is so much going on. The counsellor will be called on to provide a safe and trusting environment in which George will feel free enough to move around within his emotional shock. His feelings become accepted and acceptable, and therefore contained and containable within the therapeutic relationship. In this there is the seed of hope that they can be contained outside as well. George will then be more likely to be able to see through his confusion, refocus himself and begin to make realistic decisions concerning his future alcohol use.

HAVE I GOT A PROBLEM?

George may be wanting an answer to the question, 'Have I got a problem?' The counsellor may respond by indicating his or her sense of how important it is for him to know: 'You desperately want to know if your alcohol use has become a problem in itself.' George may then wish to explore why, or engage with his feeling of desperation.

However, George may be coming across in a much more 'matter-of-fact' manner, showing that he wants to be clear on this now so he can move on to do something about it rather than embark on a long process of exploration. The counsellor's empathic sensitivity to this may lead to a comment along the lines of: 'Well, there is no doubt that the alcohol use has caused you a problem – the drink-driving. Are you also wanting an answer as to whether it is a problem to your health and well-being?' If the answer is yes, then recommended safe drinking levels and the health effects of heavy alcohol use can be usefully conveyed to the client and time given for George to reflect on the implications of this information.

There is a place for offering information such as this within the person-centred counselling relationship. While some might argue that the counsellor is in danger of upsetting the power balance within the relationship, taking on a role of 'expert', it remains a fact that to hold back useful information or ideas is, in a sense, an abuse of the counsellor's position as a trusted person. Information is offered as something that could be helpful, and worth considering, while the counsellor endeavours to ensure that the client will feel free to accept or reject it. I take the view that while I am not an 'expert' on my client's life and process of change, I do have 'specialist' knowledge that might be of value.

> *George:* So what do you think about half a bottle of whisky four times a week?
>
> *Counsellor:* Well, I am aware that guidelines are that one bottle spread evenly across a week is above safe drinking. It leaves me concerned for your well-being.

or

> *George:* Well, I need to do something about my drinking. Any ideas?
>
> *Counsellor:* One idea that has been around a long while and which many people find helpful is keeping a drinking diary...

However, George might say: 'Well, I need to do something about my drinking. It's making me feel uncomfortable ...' The counsellor has a choice of whether to respond to the voiced need, to the discomfort, or to both. The decision will depend largely on the counsellor's empathic understanding and congruent experience of what is of the uppermost concern to George. If the counsellor does not know what this is, it is helpful to say so in order that the client can clarify this for himself.

The counsellor responding with 'You want to change your drinking, it has become too uncomfortable to continue' would leave George free to choose which way to go, as long as the counsellor watches his intonation and avoids placing more emphasis on George's wanting to change either his drinking or his discomfort. Or the counsellor could usefully voice his wondering, if it is present, by adding: 'I am wondering whether you want to explore strategies for change, or the discomfort you are feeling?' George's response might be: 'What kind of strategies?'

Then the drinking diary could be offered as one idea, or looking at what currently encourages drinking and what could limit the need or the opportunity could be suggested. If George does seek change, there are many areas to explore. How might he use the time he now has? Are there other interests that he might develop? What led him to the choices he has made to fill his time, and obstructed him from other options? For him to change his drinking pattern will involve other changes to his lifestyle and routine. Social contact may be important, though probably more difficult with the loss of his driving licence. Voluntary work, creative interests, activities that not only fill his time but also give him a sense of being useful and valued may be considered. He has talked of his low mood; this could become lower the longer he drifts along doing very little and blurring his feelings with alcohol.

However, this may not be what is needed immediately. George may need more time to understand why he has been using alcohol. Has he a history of loss, with alcohol use as his prime coping mechanism? Is there a high sensitivity within him towards the feelings that arise in relation to loss or loneliness that sends him into an almost 'automatic-pilot' drinking-mode? This is not unusual, particularly with issue-based binge-drinkers. The anticipated loss of his licence could exacerbate feelings he has struggled with for most of his life.

Openness

Clients with drinking problems often raise the question of whether they should tell other people, friends and relatives who are not aware. How open should they be about it? If they are open, how should they describe themselves? A 'person with a drink problem' is simplest to accept, yet whom do they trust enough to tell? This is a real dilemma. I am of the opinion that there is much to be gained from openness, from being honest with people, but there can be fear of ridicule, or of people being upset by the disclosure: the parent who will blame themselves when their son or daughter reveals an alcohol problem. Yet when it is in the open the tension and stress of trying to hide the secret diminishes. Each person must make their own decision.

Disclosure to friends and relatives can help to reduce the likelihood of being pressured into having a drink as long as those who are told accept it. Those who themselves are problematic drinkers may feel threatened by it, and thereby become a threat to the client's attempts at change. I have heard it said: 'Well, you certainly find out who your friends are. The moment I mentioned I was cutting back I got seriously ridiculed. It made me feel so small. I really struggled to say no, but I achieved it. What's wrong with them?' The truth is that often the people who make it most difficult are the heavy drinking acquaintances, friends or relatives who themselves cannot control their alcohol intake.

Christmas and New Year are particularly difficult times, as are other parties and family occasions. What if people are not aware that a person is trying to be abstinent? Can that person deal with the 'go on, have one, it's Christmas', that can go on for hours. How will they cope with the simple availability of large quantities of alcohol, and the air of expectation that they should have a drink? They may fear being unable to enjoy themselves, or of missing out.

Sometimes the difficulty is more around 'who knows'. Has a partner or a relation told other people in the family, or not? It can become the topic nobody talks about, creating awkwardness and anxiety. Alternatively, some people will broadcast it to everyone in a highly condemnatory way, thinking they can shame the drinker into not drinking. Often this has the opposite effect, feeding the shame that already exists and perhaps ensuring it reaches that unbearable point at which drinking occurs. The unhelpful broadcast of 'Whatever you do, don't give Angie a drink, she's an alcoholic' may be well-meaning, or it may be said in a manner that is intended to belittle, giving the speaker a sense of power over another human being. It can provoke a fight-back, the weapon being the alcohol, as in this case Angie decides to assert her sensed right to choose a drink. Often it will end in disaster; the trap has been set and Angie, in her outrage, has fallen into it.

So, while openness is generally the best way forward, in some situations this can generate more stress, the problematic drinker facing difficult decisions about which relationships are going to prove valuable in their endeavours to change. When I am asked about this I generally say that most people find it more helpful to be honest, but that the client often needs to think it through for themselves in the context of their own lives. I am always ready to explore this so that a client can reach a decision that is right for them at that time. Of course, I am also aware that people change, and a need for secrecy today may become a need for greater openness tomorrow.

Planning change

Scenario 6

> *Michael is 35 years old. After four counselling sessions he has himself come to the realization that he is drinking too much and he wants to cut back. Currently he has a couple of pints over lunch in the pub round the corner from where he works, a couple of cans of lager when he arrives home to unwind, three or four glasses of wine with an evening meal most days, an occasional drink when*

watching television in the evening and a couple of trips to the pub each week in the evening, usually for two or three pints.

Michael has made a decision to cut back and is looking for strategies to achieve this. Some of his drinking is at home, some social. Some is designed to enable him to relax and unwind, some is in association with other activities. The reality is that he is drinking a minimum of ten units a day, some days much more. He is certainly above safe drinking and there is a high likelihood of physical damage if this continues. What changes might be planned?

The first thing for the counsellor to try to help Michael recognize is which parts of his daily drinking pattern he feels would be easiest to change, and which most difficult. He may immediately see which to tackle first. If not, then a simple process of working through each drinking experience one by one can help him to clarify which he might begin to reduce. For Michael, drinking during the lunch break could be difficult for him to change if this is a social experience with colleagues who are all heavy drinkers. Considering this might lead him to want to explore why this is so, what his friendships mean to him and how they impact on his sense of self and behaviour. The likelihood of change could also depend on his friends and how they are likely to react.

There might be a non-drinker in the group with whom Michael could join in having an alcohol-free alternative, thereby making this change easier. He may go on his own sometimes to the pub and, therefore, an alternative lunch-time activity might be considered, or going somewhere else to eat. Remember we are dealing with someone who wants to change; he will not be in denial of the problem, or blocking the ideas discussed. He will need time to weigh up his options. He will know what is realistic, what he can see himself doing, and what change he feels is impossible to contemplate.

It might be the drink when he gets home that he feels he could cut out. One tip is for him to make sure an alternative drink is visible, available and accessible when he comes in. It could make the difference between getting a can of lager out of the refrigerator or clicking on a kettle that is waiting and full of water. Maybe the cans would be best kept in a cupboard, or even not bought, if that is possible. When are they bought, and by whom? Could he reduce the strength, or take them as a shandy to reduce the number of cans consumed?

The drink while watching television may be Michael's reward for a hectic day. What is the drink – a large scotch that is a home measure (probably a double or treble), or a can of lager (the stronger cans are four or more units each), or is it a small can of beer, perhaps not more than a unit? Often this kind of drinking is habit. Can he get into the habit of an alternative drink? Always encourage a range of options rather than one replacement, because people may get bored with it, which puts them at risk of a relapse. People never seem to get bored with a favourite alcoholic drink.

What about the trips to the pub? He wants some social contact, but is the pub his only option? He may never have thought of going anywhere else, or developing some other evening activity with other people. Often a change of social life is called for.

However, some people can maintain a pub-based social life without a return to heavy alcohol use. People who have spent many years drinking in favourite pubs do genuinely experience them as places that feel like home, full of people who are friends, who are pleased to see them, with whom they can laugh and joke. They can be places where they get a great sense of satisfaction that may be hard to replace. Could Michael see himself switching to a low alcohol beer, or even to something non-alcoholic in the pub?

Wine with a meal is a very pleasant experience, but does Michael need three or four glasses? Maybe he is sharing with a partner and they generally do not leave unfinished bottles. In this case, Michael is more likely to be able to go for the odd meal without wine at all than to try to part-drink a bottle and leave the rest for another day. If Michael does think he can cork the bottle half-full, maybe he can also have a jug of water on the table so there is a greater chance of less wine being consumed.

Maybe he could cut back to a couple of glasses of wine. What sort of wine is it? Is it low quality, so there is less of an interest in the flavour, more in the effect? Sometimes switching to a quality wine can change the drinking experience and reduce the intake, because it is being drunk for its flavour accompanying the meal. A subtle change of habit like that can also mirror a change in self-concept. 'You know, I really am beginning to think I deserve something better than the bottles of plonk I drank previously. I can really get satisfaction from a couple of glasses of good wine. I never gave myself the chance in the past, it never touched the sides, or my taste buds.'

Approaching the issue in this way can make the whole process more manageable and much more likely to succeed than the client going off with a vague notion of cutting back but without any clearly defined plan or awareness of the drinking pattern. It gives more manageable elements to work with and offers greater scope for a successful outcome.

RESPONDING TO DEPENDENCE

If the cans Michael is drinking when he gets home and when watching television are strong lagers, his daily intake could be as high as 20 units. Over a long enough period this is going to induce physical dependence. Has he been drinking to this pattern for some while? The lunch-time drinking may be to stave off withdrawal reactions. Does he feel anxious, perhaps a little shaky towards the end of the morning, or a little panicky and on edge prior to that lunch-time drink? If he is drinking to this level and withdrawal symptoms are present, he will need to reduce slowly and, if he chooses to try to stop altogether, will need to seek medical advice from his doctor or from alcohol services and will probably need medication to counteract withdrawal effects.

It is worth emphasizing that if a client who is known to be a dependent drinker tells the counsellor that he or she stopped yesterday and is feeling rough today, that client is best advised to seek medical advice as soon as possible. As an alcohol counsellor, I have spoken to people on the phone who have stopped, who are experiencing severe withdrawal symptoms and who cannot get to a doctor, and advised them to have a drink, make an appointment and come in to discuss a way to plan their change in a realistic and sustainable way. You cannot take risks with alcohol withdrawal, it may be life-threatening. Before medication was available, one in five people died during alcohol detoxification in the sanatoriums of the nineteenth century.

ACTION PLANNING DIALOGUE

Let us consider some dialogue for working with Michael. Bear in mind this is not so much a therapeutic exchange at this point as a working together to formulate ideas for taking action in response to Michael's decision to cut back on his drinking.

Michael: I've decided that I have to cut back. I'm the only one who can make that decision, but I'm really not too sure what will be the best way to approach it.

Counsellor: That sounds pretty clear to me, uncertainty of the best way to approach it.

Michael: Yes. I mean, the lunch-time drink, well, it would be difficult to stop that. All my mates are there and everyone drinks.

Counsellor: All your mates are there, everyone drinks. No non-drinkers to attach yourself to?

Michael: No.

Counsellor: Do you drink in rounds, or can you buy your own and control it a little that way? Or maybe switch to halves instead of pints?

Michael: No. I can't see it happening.

Counsellor: OK. You can't see it happening. So what are the options to reduce at other times?

Michael: I do like a drink to unwind when I get home.

Counsellor: So, you currently like that drink to unwind. Ever found yourself missing out on it, or having something else?

Michael: A couple of years back I always had a pot of tea. My partner had it ready for me. She gets back after I do now, a couple of cans seems a lot easier somehow.

Counsellor: I'm wondering whether you need those cans of lager. Are they strong ones?

Michael: No, only five per cent. Do I need them? I don't know. I feel as though I do.

Counsellor: I guess I'm wondering whether it is a need or a habit that you've got into.

Michael: I'm not sure. But it's so much easier to open a can than mess around making tea.

Counsellor: OK, you want to take the simple option.

Michael: Yes ... well, no. I want to cut back. The simple option is so easy but I have to make other choices if I am going to change.

Counsellor: So another choice might be having the tea-making stuff left out ready for when you get home: kettle filled, teapot next to it, mug out ready.

Michael: Well, it's usually all put away. I never think about it. Maybe it might just happen, not every day; I might be able to make tea if it was easily available.

Counsellor: OK, so maybe that is an option.

Michael: Yes, the more I think about it, the more I can see those cans as a habit. I drink tea at work, and coffee, and I enjoy it.

Counsellor: So you know you enjoy tea and coffee at work but you've got out of the habit of drinking it when you get home?

Michael: Yes, I can try that. It doesn't seem too dramatic or out of my reach, and yet it will take a few units off my weekly intake. I'll give it a go next week. I'll have to explain what I'm doing to my partner. That shouldn't be a problem.

Counsellor: OK, so you're going to make that your goal for this week. Break up the pattern of using alcohol to unwind when you get home.

Michael: Do you think that's enough to be aiming for?

Counsellor: You want to aim for a greater reduction?

Michael: I'm not sure. I don't want to fail in what I set out to achieve.

Counsellor: You want to make it realistic but also ensure that you get a sense of achievement. It is often wise to go slowly and feel that you are setting yourself a goal that you believe is attainable.

Michael: Yes. I guess I'm feeling caught between wanting to cut back more and being afraid I might not be able to cut back at all.

Counsellor: That's a scary place to be, not sure what to go for.

Michael: Yeah.

(*Silence in which Michael is clearly working inwardly on his dilemma.*)

Michael: No. I'll go for this one step at a time. I do not need that drink when I get home.

Counsellor: You do not need that drink. You really are determined to break that home-from-work drink habit.

Michael: Yes, I am. It's what I want to do.

Counsellor: OK, so take it one day at a time. Don't forget, the habit's been around for a while. You may be tempted, particularly if the day is extra stressful or the journey home is bad.

Michael: Yeah, those are going to make it harder, I need to think about that. But I know I do not need that drink. I am sure it is purely habit. I've just got to get out of it.

Counsellor: It's a habit you know you've got to break out of.

Michael: Yeah. What if I do have a can when I get home, though?

Counsellor: What do you feel will happen?

Michael: I don't know. At the time, I guess I'll just want it. I'll probably feel disappointed and angry, and bad about it afterwards.

Counsellor: Any idea how you might handle those feelings?

Michael: I guess I might drink on them.

Counsellor: Disappointment, anger at yourself, feeling bad about it, and the alcohol would attract you.

Michael: But it isn't a solution. I know that. If I do drink, I need to understand why.

Counsellor: You need to understand why.

Michael: Yeah, I've got to make sense of it. I need to monitor what's happening for me.

Counsellor: Perhaps you need to see it as one day at a time. If you have that can when you come home one day, then try again the next day. You might decide to keep a track of it in the drinking diary as well – it might help us to understand what it is about particular days that makes it easier to avoid opening those cans, and what makes it harder.

I see this kind of dialogue as an application of the person-centred approach to the stage of action planning. It demonstrates how the person-centred counsellor can keep within Michael's frame of reference yet at the same time offer ideas. This gives Michael freedom to choose. The counsellor is seeking to be empathic to Michael's inner world, his concerns, his hopes, his dilemma. Michael is not being told what to do, or being pushed where he feels unable to go. However, he is being offered ideas, based on the counsellor's specialist knowledge, past experience and a sense of what is realistic, that may be helpful for him.

RAISING THE POSSIBILITY OF RELAPSE

It is often difficult to introduce to the client who is feeling positive the possibility of relapsing from what is being attempted and how this might be handled. When I feel within myself that a client is over-confident and not really thinking it through, it can be helpful to voice this. It will be based on a genuine concern that I am experiencing for the client's well-being. The client's reaction may be anger, and an unwillingness to think about relapse. This also has to be respected, and it is understandable. Sometimes, though, insight emerges out of challenging the client who does not want to consider the need to plan, or to acknowledge the possibility of not achieving a goal. In the following example, the counsellor flags up the difficulty, allowing Michael to engage with his concerns, opening up the opportunity for discussion and exploration.

> *Michael:* I'm going to stop my lunch-time drink, and the one when I get home. That's that.
>
> *Counsellor:* You sound really clear on that, cutting lunch-time and home-from-work drinking.
>
> *Michael:* Yep. I'm in control.
>
> *Counsellor:* You're in control.
>
> *Michael:* I think so.
>
> *Counsellor:* You think you are in control.
>
> *Michael:* I'm determined. I'm sure I'll be OK. But I do wonder what I will do instead.
>
> *Counsellor:* I hear that, and it is a wonder I have as well.
>
> *Michael:* I'll think of something, don't you worry.

Counsellor: I'm feeling concerned. I want you to succeed, and it can be useful to plan ahead to minimize the risk of not achieving your goal.

Michael: So you think I'm going to fail. Nobody believes in me. It comes to something when even your counsellor hasn't any faith in you.

Counsellor: You don't feel I have faith in you. It seems as if nobody believes in you. I'm concerned. I have faith in you. I want you to achieve your reduction, and I know you do.

Michael: I'll show you.

Counsellor: I'm sure you will. I respect how important it is for you to do it your own way.

(*Silence. Counsellor feels an overwhelming sense of wanting Michael to do it for himself.*)

Counsellor: I want you to do it for you.

(*This leads to a lengthy silence.*)

Michael (quietly): I never do things for me. I do things for others yet I hate being told what to do.

This scenario may then lead to a deeper exploration of Michael's behaviour pattern and sense of self. Clearly, something deeply significant has emerged. Michael was fighting back against following someone else's advice (the counsellor's), a significant move away from how he now realizes he usually operates. The counsellor's congruent voicing of what they experienced in themselves has touched something deep in Michael. He has moved in the session from only acknowledging his determination to change to connecting with another part of himself that has genuine self-doubt, which probably needs to be heard and resolved by Michael as part of his process of preparing for change in his drinking. His fuller experiencing and acceptance of himself will ensure that his determination to change will be more likely to succeed. He may now begin to accept himself as a person who can do things for himself and will think before doing what others suggest.

Change is stressful and people do not like to think of failure, yet it is important if possible for the clients to prepare themselves for risky situations and ways of handling them if they take the drink they were planning not to have. However, the client will make their own choices, and may well want to try it their way. Clients can do better than expected, they are not doomed to fail because they have not wanted to talk about relapse, or undertaken detailed planning. In my experience, though, it can be helpful to get the message over that, if things do go wrong or get difficult, there are ways of keeping in contact so that the risk of a relapse happening or getting out of control is minimized.

Scenario 7

> *Kirsty is 20 years old and has attended one previous counselling session at her college. She had spent most of the session talking about her life at college and what she wants to do with herself when she leaves. She had referred herself because she was feeling stressed by exams. She drinks spirits, but always with a mixer, never neat. She goes out most evenings and sometimes goes to the college bar at lunch time, particularly at weekends. She reckons she has between six and eight single spirits most days, a little more when she goes to parties. She wants to reduce.*

Kirsty is aware of her drinking pattern and wants to do something about it. The reasons behind her heavy drinking may need to be explored. Is it simply a matter of being part of the culture of college life? She may be using alcohol to cope specifically with being at college, or the pressure she feels under.

Is alcohol the cause of the pressure, lowering her quality of functioning and taking time that might otherwise be used for course work? Is there a separation/loss issue about being away from home that alcohol is anaesthetizing? She may see alcohol as the cause of problems, or as a coping mechanism, or both.

If it is simply a habit she has got into within the drinking culture, she may be looking either to disengage from that culture to some degree and seek out alternative interests on some of the days when she would otherwise be drinking, or to switch away from the spirits, perhaps alternating her drinks with non-alcoholic ones. The good thing is that she is mixing the spirits and not drinking them neat. This dilutes the alcohol, which will reduce its inflammatory effect. It also means she is not becoming accustomed to a strong, alcohol flavour. Perhaps she can drink the mixer on its own at the start of a session of drinking to reduce the overall total.

If Kirsty is drinking to cope with the pressure more than as part of the social scene, she may want to look at her own boundaries of working, or whether her work needs rescheduling in some way. A discussion with a tutor may be necessary to look at the workload. However, it could be that the stress is the effect of the drinking and so it would come back to breaking up the daily drinking habit. She may wish to seek a couple of dry days in the week. That would be a good start; it would enable her to have an experience of the contrast between a day after heavy drinking and one after no alcohol. This, in itself, could add to her motivation to cut back. It would also give her the time she may require to undertake the course work and therefore minimize the stress and her perceived need to drink.

THE CLIENT FINDS HER OWN EMPHASIS

Feeling heard and understood is likely to be important for Kirsty. Offering this is at the heart of the person-centred approach to counselling. When a person is in distress or confused they can feel very alone, and very much the only person with the problem. They can gain strength from having that other person (the counsellor) touching and witnessing their inner world, validating their experience and enabling them to explore more painful areas, or engaging with the confusion and offering the opportunity for fresh insight and understanding to emerge.

Kirsty: I really want to change my drinking. I know it helps me relax a bit, but I need some strategies because there has to be another way.

Counsellor: You need some strategies to replace the alcohol use.

Kirsty: Yeah, but I get so stressed. Those gin and tonics really help me take my mind off the exams.

Counsellor: They help you to stop thinking ...

Kirsty: ... Yes, about everything, a real escape. But, oh, I mean, I shouldn't need to use alcohol to unwind, should I?

Counsellor (sensing Kirsty's discomfort): It leaves you with a lot of discomfort knowing you are doing this?

Kirsty: More unsettled than discomfort. I don't know, I just seem to spend so much time in the bar. At the time it seems great, but then I find myself just thinking about it, feeling a bit grim and wondering was it all worth it.

Counsellor: Wondering ...

Kirsty: Yeah, wondering if I'm cut out for this studying. I don't know.

Counsellor: 'I don't know' seems to really capture where you are at the moment.

(*Long but working silence*)

Kirsty (*quietly*): I never really wanted to come to college, I hate being away from home. I don't know why I'm here.

Kirsty has taken herself to a place where she can engage with, and share, her dislike of being away from home. She has not been directed to this, but has been heard: this has allowed her to probe into the meaning of her 'I don't know'. Alcohol has not been a factor in the second half of this dialogue. Even though she may be wanting to plan change, keeping only to this could stifle her in engaging with, and exploring, her underlying feelings. Sometimes the planning has to be put to one side. The client is in another place. Other factors are emerging that need to be engaged with and the counsellor is called on to trust that this is both necessary and timely.

It will be helpful for Kirsty to be clear as to the root of her drinking and to experience the counsellor's support for her as a pressured person seeking to make change. A further exploration of her dislike of being away from home will run parallel with her endeavour to put any plan into action that is formulated to deal with the alcohol use. An holistic perspective is required to set the drinking in context and therefore to ensure that planned change is realistic. The greater the accuracy of the counsellor's sensing and communicating of Kirsty's inner (and outer) world, the more self-affirming she will be. The counsellor has to be not only empathic to the person, but also to the situation he or she is in, the life-context, of which the drinking is one feature.

It is therapeutically valuable to allow the client to trust their own evaluation of their situation. This is a crucial step towards the client shifting their locus of evaluation, taking it away from being invested in the opinions of others, and increasingly becoming centred within their own experience. Time with a person-centred counsellor to plan and receive support for change in her drinking, coupled with an exploration of her feelings and thoughts towards being at college, will offer Kirsty the opportunity to confront and more fully understand the behaviour patterns and choices she is making. She will move towards a fuller and more satisfying engagement with her own autonomy, freeing herself from conditional 'configurations' or the living out of, or reaction against, other people's agendas.

Taking action

Following on from a period of planning change will come putting the plan into action. It will be important that there is a clear time frame, so that it is not always going to begin 'next week'; that there is a way of tracking the drinking if it is a planned reduction (use the drinking diary); that it is owned by the client and is seen by them as realistic; that support is organized as much as possible and that the risks of lapse or relapse have been explored and ways of dealing with them discussed.

In a sense, the action phase is quite short. The client has made his or her decision, planned what to do, and goes off and attempts it. The moment of taking action is worthy of focus, however, because like the decision to change, the act of change is an important pivotal point within the client's world. The client is now fully engaged with their motivation to change. Any ambivalence has been explored and worked through. It could be said that they have entered into a more congruent state with regard to their alcohol use. They have greater clarity as to why they drink, and they know why they are seeking to change their drinking pattern. Anxieties that they have concerning change will, it is hoped, have been identified during the contemplation and planning phase.

Fresh sense of self emerges

While it is a time of anxiety, taking action also releases some extremely positive feelings. It is as if an aspect of the person's nature is struggling to free itself from an habitual and conditioned response to circumstances, this response being the alcohol use, or the reactions that lead to it (for instance, when a person provokes arguments to give themselves an excuse to go out and get drunk). Freeing themselves from configurations of self that are rooted in past negative conditioning releases creative and developmental 'energy'.

It is as though an aspect of the person, that they have lost touch with, begins to assert itself once more. A kind of shaking off of conditioning takes place as the person enters into greater authenticity in their inner world of self-experience and expression. We see here the presence of the actualizing tendency moving the person towards a fuller sense of self. They are engaging with aspects of their nature that perhaps have been lost for a long time, or new features within their redefined self-concept that bring a sense of satisfaction and which reflect movement towards fuller functionality. It is empowering. The person can experience a sense of feeling more complete.

Many clients describe this in terms of it being a spiritual experience: 'It's not the language I would expect to hear myself using, but it really does feel spiritual, a sort of "high" and yet it is more about feeling whole than being high'. Clients who achieve their goal during the action phase generally come back with a sense of achievement, with a greater sense of self-satisfaction coupled with an urge to grow even more into this newly found way of being.

While the movement of the clients' locus of evaluation is deeply satisfying and liberating, anxiety can arise when they are faced with a situation in which old patterns echo within them, or the voice of the person whom they have always listened to causes them to hesitate and be tempted towards self-doubt.

It is important to have in mind that the act of reducing alcohol intake, or of stopping, could be the first time a client has consciously and intentionally pursued a course of action, for their own benefit, of their own volition. To put it another way, they may be acting out of a newly formed configuration of self that is rooted in self-acceptance and positive self-regard, not in old configurations shaped by negative conditioning. It can be a genuine act of reclaiming power. It can make an enormous impression and the risk is that it generates a 'high' which leads to complacency. The client cannot afford to drop their guard, they have stepped into what is, for them, an unknown situation – life without alcohol, or life without alcohol in association with certain activities, feelings, or routines.

For some clients, a change of alcohol habit does not bring relief and release, but a sense of being less able to cope. The loss is too overwhelming. This could be because so much of the person's normality is centred on alcohol use and the step away from it is too great to take at the time, or it may be that chemically the body is out of balance to a significant degree. They may experience extreme anxiety, or depression, with relapse a very real possibility. Medical intervention may be necessary to help the person stabilize while counselling continues.

Scenario 8

> Liz decided at the last session that she was going to be dry for the whole of the following week. A lot of planning and gradual reduction had led up to this. She had tended to drink in the evenings; she is a single parent with two young children and a busy schedule during the day.

Counsellor: So, how has the week worked out?

Liz: I'm dry!

Counsellor: You look really pleased with yourself, and I sense some disbelief as well.

Liz: Yeah. I know I had planned it carefully (*note the 'I', an important indicator of ownership of the process*) but there was always that wonder as to whether I could do it.

Counsellor: So you had been wondering right the way through whether you could stop, but you have and it was your plan that worked.

Liz: Yes, well, I did have some help (*with a smile*).

Counsellor: We worked at it together but you're the one who really planned it and has put it into practice.

Liz: Yeah. It feels good although I have had a few shaky moments.

Counsellor: So generally it has been a good experience but there have been times that have been difficult.

Liz: Yes. A couple of times I've phoned friends in the evening. It was a good idea sellotaping phone numbers of people I could speak to by the phone. I didn't have to think, just dial the number.

Counsellor: Was it a craving to drink, or some other feeling that was making it risky?

Liz: Oh, it was when the children were in bed, you know, that time for me when I used to drink (*another powerful affirmation*), I could feel that itchy, nagging urge coming at me.

Counsellor: That's when you made the phone call?

Liz: Yes, and had a couple of sugary sweets as well, as we'd discussed. After a while it went away. You know, I'd never

ever not drunk on that feeling in the past; I never realized it could pass without having a drink.

Counsellor: Sounds as if you have learned some really important things, and found you can make different choices.

Liz: Yes, I feel great.

Maybe after a couple more sessions with Liz maintaining abstinence, a comment might be made such as:

Liz: So, do I still need to see you? I really feel I've cracked it.

Counsellor: You're very confident; however, it is just three weeks dry. My experience tells me that it is good to keep regular contact to ensure that the new lifestyle really is firmly established.

Liz: Oh. You mean, you don't think I'm OK then?

Counsellor: I think you have done really well, and I really want to be sure that nothing upsets what you have achieved. I really hear your motivation to stay dry, and I am mindful of the discussions we had in the past over relapse prevention: I really want to keep that message alive.

Liz: Hmm.

Counsellor: Sounds as if you really didn't want to hear that.

Liz: No, you're right, I really am still learning this non-drinking thing.

Counsellor: Maybe you're right as well, that you want to move on. Change is powerful, isn't it?

Liz: Yes. It feels good to be in control.

Counsellor: Feeling in control sounds kind of a new experience?

Liz: Yeah, and I want more of it.

Counsellor: You want more control. It leaves me wondering how your urge for greater control impacts on our relationship and the counselling sessions? (*Voiced from a genuine experience of this wondering within the counsellor.*)

Liz: Well, I suppose I'm really aware of who makes me feel controlled now because I feel that resistance thing when I'm being pushed.

Counsellor: And I just pushed you into thinking about something you didn't want to think about.

Liz: That's about it. I guess it's left me very sensitive and I've kind of swung to the other extreme – I don't want anyone pushing me around and telling me what to do.

Counsellor: That sounds really strong; don't push me around, don't tell me what to do.

Liz: That's right, but then I guess it can also stop me listening to others as well. I'm really finding out some stuff about myself.

Counsellor: So being strong, being in control can make it hard for you to listen to others …

Liz: And to hear advice when it clashes with what I want.

Such an exchange is not uncommon and in this instance is opening up some interesting areas Liz may wish to explore. Clients in action are going to discover facets of themselves which are new to them, and which are going to test them out within the counselling relationship. It can be helpful to enable them to see what is happening. In this dialogue, the tendency to swing across to an extreme is noted. This is a tendency often present in people with alcohol problems, struggling to find balance when they are used to life being like an emotional see-saw. Part of the relapse prevention message is to enable the client to be aware of this so that they can anticipate some swings during the change and after. Carrying an awareness of this possibility is an aid to finding balance.

Having made the change, the next challenge for any client is to maintain it. The counsellor offers to support this, seeking to help minimize relapse as well as offering an opportunity for the client to explore how they are feeling about their new life-style, and how they may wish to develop it further.

Key points

- Not everyone is prepared to change.
- Clear advice and information provide the opportunity for an informed decision.
- People may spend a long time thinking about change before taking action.
- Any planned change in a drinking pattern must be realistic and owned by the client.
- Raising the issue of relapse during action planning is helpful and may be challenging to the client.
- Clients generally find that achieving their goal is a powerful experience.

CHAPTER 6

Maintaining Change and Responding to Relapse

When someone changes a habit, how long is it before the changed pattern can truly be said to be an established part of their normal routine and lifestyle? This will vary from person to person – perhaps six months, possibly shorter, probably longer. Throughout that time there is always a risk of lapsing, or relapsing, so at this stage much of the focus is on minimizing the risk of this occurring and ensuring that support systems to help sustain the change are being maintained.

Some people will exit maintenance after a while, pleased with what they have achieved and free to move on in their life. Others will feel empowered, begin to question other habits or patterns and will contemplate new changes. Some clients, however, may feel they need to continue watching their changed pattern for a lot longer and it may be a while before they really feel free from having to put energy into maintaining their change. Others will experience a relapse.

The maintenance phase

The maintenance phase may bring up a range of difficulties for clients. One that often occurs is that clients do not want to keep in contact during this period, particularly when things are going well. They feel that they have made their change and no longer need the counsellor. If the counsellor is experiencing concerns about this, they need to be discussed in a manner that does not undermine the client.

Scenario 9

> *Barry has been maintaining a change in his alcohol use for a couple of months.*
>
> *Barry:* Well, it is nearly eight weeks since my last drink. I think I'm OK now. I don't see much point in coming to you any more.
>
> *Counsellor:* So you are feeling OK about ending the counselling sessions.
>
> *Barry:* Yes. I'm in control now.
>
> *Counsellor:* Great. You're in control. So how would you like to use this session?
>
> *Barry:* I guess I'd like to review what I have gained, and maybe talk about what I might do next.
>
> *Counsellor:* OK. Where do you want to start?

The counsellor has accepted Barry's decision and has offered him time to set his own agenda for the session. Any concerns the counsellor may have are noted, but are not being voiced. Barry is being left to trust his own instincts, an important feature of the person-centred approach. As the session progresses, and as Barry experiences the counsellor's acceptance of his decision, he decides to reveal that he actually does have some concerns himself:

> *Barry:* Talking to you with the ending coming along, it does feel a bit scary. It's what I want to do, and I realize it is a big step.

Counsellor: So while you wish to end, it leaves you with some anxiety.

Barry: Yes. Am I going to end too soon? Will I be OK? I really feel that I will be, and yet, there is the unknown. I don't want another relapse. I cannot keep coming, I need to prove to myself that I can be independent.

Counsellor: You want to be independent of counselling; you also don't want another relapse.

Barry: So do you think I should continue?

Counsellor: You really want to hear my opinion? I cannot make the decision for you. I trust your instinct to end counselling, and I am aware it is only eight weeks. While from your perspective that seems a long time, it is a short period to be sure that change has taken root.

Barry: Part of me feels that way, and I know I came in saying I was OK and ready to end; I know this other part of me feels I need a bit of a safety net or something in case I slip.

Counsellor: You want to end and you want to have a safety net.

Barry: Any ideas? Can I see you less frequently, or something?

The discussion might then explore the length of the counselling sessions, their frequency or their focus. Some clients may want to 'check in' for half an hour every couple of weeks. There is a case for flexibility and letting the client consider options beyond the therapeutic hour that may not have been something they had thought about. What the above dialogue also highlights is that as Barry has been allowed to feel that his choice has been accepted, he is then able to voice those doubts that he carries as well. He has changed his mind during the session, not because he has been persuaded to by the counsellor, but because he has allowed himself to be in touch with and voice his own feelings concerning his decision.

Barry may now be less preoccupied with thinking about not drinking, and ready to move on to greater independence. While for Barry the 'therapeutic hour' was a highlight within his isolated week, he has now moved on. It had been his one opportunity to have space, to feel valued and worthy as a human being, to be able to share his inner world without fear of judgement or rejection, and to find support and encouragement. Now he is engaging in a wide range of interests during his week. How the client uses the rest of his or her time contributes enormously to the therapeutic process. (The counselling contact is only one hour out of 168 in a week, or 336 in a fortnight.) If clients develop other interests and activities that express the new configurations of self that are increasingly becoming a feature of their 'self-acceptance', that enable them to feel freed up as a person, valued and useful, the significance of the therapeutic hour can be reduced significantly. The importance of the counselling relationship diminishes as they grow away from past conditioning, enabling them to establish a lifestyle that will bring greater satisfaction to their new sense of self.

Taking the same scenario, it could be that Barry's motive for ending is explored:

Barry: Well, it is nearly eight weeks since my last drink. I think I'm OK now. I don't see much point in coming to you any more.

Counsellor: You're feeling ready to end the counselling sessions then?

Barry: Yes. I mean, I am sure there are others who need to see you more than I do.

Counsellor: So I am left wondering whether you are wanting to end the sessions because you feel ready to move on, or because you feel you are taking up someone else's time who you feel may be in greater need, or maybe both? What is best for you?

This is clearly heading in a different direction and may well lead to work on Barry's self-worth. Does he genuinely feel ready to move on, in which case the person-centred perspective will trust that he is, or is he saying this but feeling he is not worth more time even though he needs it? As the emphasis is placed on allowing Barry to choose what is best for him, he is left with a sense of having confidence placed in him, of being heard, and I believe a better chance of making his thoughts and feelings visible in the session and/or making the decision that is right for him at that time.

Scenario 10

> *Always a heavy drinker, Phil took to problematic drinking following being made redundant at age 55. As the weeks passed Phil found himself in the pub more and more and it got to the point where he was drinking in the mornings at home as well to stave off withdrawal symptoms. The plan was for him to go through detoxification (which was successful), give himself a dry period and then review the situation. It is now six weeks since the detoxification.*

Phil will need to have planned activities to fill his days. Getting a job will have been his main focus for using his time. However, as time drags by, job-seeking gets harder, and without something to fill his time and engage him in a fulfilling manner, sustainable change will be unlikely. So during the period in which he is seeking to maintain change, it may be important to check out how the job search is affecting him, and what else he might do to give himself some sense of satisfaction. It may be that everything is fine, that he is keeping busy and making what he feels to be good use of his time, taking up new interests and making new friends.

Yet he could be feeling dissatisfied with his new interests and beginning to think back to the social benefits of drinking and how it had helped him get away from his difficulties in finding work. It is important that Phil is offered a therapeutic climate in which his fears and struggles can be present, heard and accepted, by the counsellor and by Phil. If he feels unable to express his fears, if he tries to suppress his feelings, the discomfort will build up, leading to a very real possibility of lapse or relapse.

In the following dialogue, a 'drinking dream' has unsettled Phil.

Phil: I don't know, it just doesn't feel right somehow.

Counsellor: It doesn't feel right?

Phil: Well, I don't feel right. I'm finding it hard to keep motivated. I feel I'm missing out.

Counsellor: Motivation is a struggle, and you're missing out?

Phil: Missing out on seeing people. I've stopped going to the pub as we agreed, but now I've stopped the AA meetings as well. Just keep thinking: 'What's the point?'

Counsellor: AA was something that you had been really motivated to do, but somehow it has slipped away from you.

Phil: Yes. I just felt so awkward at the meetings, didn't know what to say to people, you know. Just felt that a drink would have relaxed me, calmed me down a bit.

Counsellor: So you're struggling with the social bit; you are feeling anxious, and something is reminding you that a drink might help.

Phil: Yes, and it is getting harder to ignore it. I was really tempted last Monday. I'd woken up feeling very shaky. This'll sound daft, but I had a really vivid dream, left me thinking I'd had a drink.

Counsellor: Have you had many of these dreams?

Phil: A few, since the detoxification. But this one was so real, really left me shaky.

Counsellor: Vivid stuff…

Phil: Too right.

It is likely that at this point I would say something about drinking dreams. I find clients who have not heard of them generally find it helpful to know they are not unusual, and that they are the kind of symptoms than can arise. This is specialist knowledge that I wish to pass on to the client.

Counsellor: It sounds as though you are experiencing drinking dreams.

Phil: 'Drinking dream' you say, damn good name for it.

Counsellor: Drinking dreams are not uncommon, and can leave people with a real belief that they have had a drink. The dreams are always extremely vivid and difficult to distinguish from reality; they can leave you experiencing physical symptoms.

Phil: Too right. I really felt as though I'd had a drink. So I'm not going mad then?

Counsellor: No. But I bet you've not only been shaky, but sweating too, and maybe feeling a bit hungover after the dream?

Phil: Yeah, and that's what's really odd. I never had hangovers when I was drinking. It doesn't seem fair.

Counsellor: It doesn't seem fair. Eight weeks dry and here you are dreaming of drinking alcohol and being left feeling worse than when you were drinking.

Phil: I guess it's why I'm saying 'What's the point?'

Counsellor: Makes you wonder why you've gone through all that you have.

Phil: Yes. (*working silence*) Well, I know why I went through it. I was drinking all day. I really don't want to go back to that, but these dreams are leaving me feeling very frightened.

Counsellor: You don't want to go back to how it was but the dreams have kind of caught you off-guard. Very frightening.

Phil: Yes. Are you sure they're normal?

Counsellor: Yes, they are common. They do pass.

Phil: Well, that's a relief.

This kind of experience is not unusual. The interaction has allowed Phil to be reassured, his fear has been heard and he has begun to reconnect with his original reason for detoxification. He may now begin to feel encouraged to work towards rediscovering his motivation. This may lead to revising the plan for change, and a consideration of ways of minimizing the risk of a relapse should similar dreams occur in the future.

Low mood after detoxification/reduction

As time passes following a detoxification or reduction in alcohol intake, the client's mood may begin to lower. Often it dips down but then comes up. There is a process of loss with the usual feelings associated with this. It can feel really strange not to be drinking, and be very tiring, particularly when the person is experiencing cravings and is using a lot of emotional and mental energy to resist the temptation.

If the mood continues to lower, or does not rise, there is a very real possibility that depression underlies the past alcohol use. Alcohol is a chemical mask. When the mask is removed, mental health issues that were previously put down simply to the effects of the alcohol use may become more present and significant. While this can be helped through the continuation of the counselling, it may also be appropriate for the client to seek medical advice. Appropriately prescribed medication may lift mood, minimize the risk of relapse and enable the client to achieve a sustainable abstinence.

Lapse and relapse

What is the difference between a 'lapse' and a 'relapse'? A lapse is more of a 'blip' than a sustained return to a past drinking pattern. The person who has been maintaining abstinence lapses, has a bad day and comes home and drinks a few beers, yet does not return to a heavy drinking pattern. Or the binge drinker, who, while still having occasional drinks in social settings, has not had an intense five-day binge for six months, may lapse one lonely weekend when things do not go right, spend two days drinking, but manage to stop much sooner than would previously have been the case.

Relapse is returning to an ingrained drinking habit as, for instance, the person who suddenly starts to take spirits again, who simply could not sustain abstinence, and is soon back into daily drinking at previous levels; or the binge drinker who returns to the old pattern in terms of both duration and quantity of drinking. Relapses are much harder to break out of; the hope is that lapses will not turn into relapses. When a client is planning for change, as we have seen earlier, the plan should include ways of dealing with a lapse to try to put a brake on it before it gets out of hand.

For the client, either a lapse or a relapse may feel as if they have gone back to square one. However, they have gone through a learning process, which may have been forgotten in the intensity of the drinking experience. A way of thinking about it is to imagine a railway track. The client gets on a train at Station A with the counsellor. The goal is to reach Station C, but the client gets off at Station B. They have not achieved their goal, but they have travelled some of the way. The fact that they have got off the train makes them feel as if they are no longer on the journey, they are back on a platform. Yet they are on a different platform at a different station. They have made part of the journey, the experiences of which can be recaptured and remembered.

It is hoped that the client will learn from the journey so far and, when the time is right, catch another train to move further up the line towards fuller functionality and a more fulfilling, less alcohol-reliant/dependent lifestyle.

From a person-centred perspective lapse or relapse can be seen in some cases as an effect of the self-concept fighting back (Mearns 1992), of an established aspect of the person's sense of self that is strongly associated with the alcohol use reasserting itself. It is as though an aspect of the person's sense of self that is still very much psychologically alive, yet which has been constrained by the will to remain abstinent or in control, breaks through bringing with it a range of familiar behaviours and attitudes. The person in effect runs out of internal resources in the struggle to maintain a change of drinking habit as an expression of their newly developing sense of self.

Configurations of self, within the self-concept, that are linked to problematic alcohol use are a major cause of lapse and relapse. This is reflected in comments such as:

> I just lost it. The 'new me' had nowhere left to hide from the pain of those old memories. There was nothing of me that I could find to fight it. 'Hurt me' overwhelmed me again. The alcohol anaesthetized 'hurt me' for a while, but I needed more, like I always did.

> Not getting that job just fed into all those old rejections. 'I'm useless' took over. I followed the old script; I drank.

> I panicked. I couldn't bear letting anyone down but I had taken on too much. It all became so intense. I needed to slow down but I couldn't. All I could think of was what I did to slow down when 'manic me' took over in the past; I drank.

In these situations the therapist is challenged to accept not only the configuration that is fighting back, but also those other developing features of the client's personality which the client has lost sight of. The risk is that the therapist colludes only with the aspect that is 'striking back' (Mearns 1992). A battle is taking place within the client's self-concept and it is a crucial time in which to maintain contact and to offer a relationship in which the core conditions are communicated.

Fear of relapse
Scenario 11

Here, John is beginning to struggle with abstinence.

John: It seems to be getting harder. I just don't seem 'me' somehow.

Counsellor: A different sense of 'me' that is unfamiliar?

John: Yes, I'm not sure that the things I'm doing to fill my time are really what I want. I'm feeling lost. When I was working I had such a clear routine, I had to stick to it. Now, well, I can choose not to, can't I? And it is really tempting not to bother. I don't like feeling this way. I kind of feel it might leave me wanting to drink.

Counsellor: Your concern is very real, 'Am I going to drink because I cannot keep to my new routines?'

John: Yes, maybe it's me, or maybe it's what I'm doing. Either way, something's not quite right.

Counsellor: So you are really unsure about what it is, but it is definitely leaving you unsettled.

John: I want to do something useful, and I really feel I need to relate to more people as well.

Counsellor: You want to 'do something useful', something that involves relating to other people.

John: Yes, it's what I want to do. You know we talked about my doing voluntary work but I felt that it wasn't me; well, I'm having second thoughts now.

Counsellor: You didn't feel that you wanted to get back into some kind of 'work'; you were retired and wanted a rest, if I remember correctly.

John: Well, I'm beginning to change my mind on it. What do you think?

Counsellor: You want to know what I think, and I'd like to hear more of what you think.

John: It feels right. I want to do something useful, use my time, get something out of it. I'm getting a lift just thinking about it.

Counsellor: And I'm sitting here feeling really good about this idea, particularly as it is something that you have thought about and are seriously considering for yourself.

John: It would need some changes to what I am doing at the moment. And I really do not know quite what is available. Maybe I can spend some time exploring this.

It is not unusual for plans to have to be adjusted. Although a client is in the maintenance phase, they are not static. They are still experiencing a process of change. Initial ideas may need revisiting. Allowing the client to own their thoughts and feelings about trying something else is important. John is being encouraged to trust his own perceptions, to affirm his internal locus of evaluation, as he struggles to discover a new sense of self.

Learning from a lapse
Scenario 12

Amanda has planned to reduce her daily intake by cutting out lunch-time drinking at work and going to the pub less with friends – the idea has been for her to organize other evening activities that are less alcohol-centred. To begin with, this had been seen by her as unthinkable; her social life had been very pub-centred. She has started going to a local gym twice a week and has made new friends through an alcohol support group. She still goes to the pub on average three nights a week, and often has a lunch-time drink at weekends. Amanda has maintained this for two months. Her alcohol intake is still a little above 'safe drinking'; however, she is feeling better in herself.

Amanda: I am feeling much more settled now. The alcohol support group really helped me to gain my confidence again, and I'm beginning to wonder whether I ought to cut back some more. My drinking is mainly at weekends. I am pleased it is less in the week, but I am concerned in case it increases.

Counsellor: You are feeling pleased and a little concerned?

Amanda: Yes, well, I did drink more than usual this last weekend. I had a row at work on Friday and had a little more than usual that evening; then I had more on Saturday and Sunday. I took the day off yesterday, I really felt groggy.

Counsellor: So the row really got to you and you made a choice to use alcohol?

Amanda: That's right. Silly really. But it has left me feeling that I need to cut back and break the weekend drinking pattern. It feels as if it leaves me at risk of going over the top.

Counsellor: It feels like a really big risk.

Amanda: Yes.

Counsellor: You don't want to put yourself at risk of going over the top?

Amanda: No, and I can feel going out for a drink at the weekends really is a habit. I am aware that I am looking forward to it in the week.

Counsellor: The thought of a drink at the weekend is with you a lot of the time?

Amanda: Not all the time, but when I feel under stress it comes to mind.

Counsellor: Mhm. Stress makes you feel like drinking.

Amanda: It leaves me thinking how good it would be to have something else to look forward to at weekends. I need to get more variety into my weekends, don't I?

Counsellor: Is that what you want?

Amanda: Yes. It's habit, like the lunch-time drinking was. I now go shopping, or go into the park for my lunch, and it's OK. I need to root out the weekend habit and having something to look forward to would be good.

Amanda has used her lapse to realize that she needs to make further changes. The developing part of her nature that wants to control the alcohol use is fighting against the established pattern and configuration that tells her, 'I am a person who uses alcohol to deal with stress, and that is a satisfying way of coping with it'. Within her maintenance she is now contemplating fresh changes in her life; we might say that the actualizing tendency is finding a focus through that aspect of herself that derives satisfaction from controlling her alcohol use and engaging with new activities and experiences. I find that empathy offers clients the opportunity to engage with ideas, or desires, that they really are drawn to. While there are times when I will share in a creative brainstorming session with clients, often it is the ideas that emerge from within their own process that prove to be most helpful in enabling the client to achieve their plan of change. It is often a time of tremendous creativity, and I can be left feeling energized by the whole process.

Working with a relapsing client

Relapse is a significant phase within the cycle of change. People do not always achieve what they set out to at the first attempt. They are drawn back into old patterns and habits. It is hard enough to break free of a habit that is simply an activity of some kind. It is even more difficult when it has involved significant chemical interactions within the body. In my experience this is often the most emotionally and mentally demanding aspect of working with people who are seeking to overcome an alcohol problem. Being part of a supportive team, and having regular supervision and support, ensures that I maintain my own psychological well-being during this challenging phase within the process of change.

Scenario 13

> *Linda is 55 years old and has re-referred. She had seen the counsellor the previous year to help her with her reduction. Then she stopped coming, saying all was OK. She had previously been drinking heavily for 15 years but last year, following the beginning of a new relationship, had decided to cut down from about four bottles of spirits a week drunk mainly during the day. She successfully contained her drinking, though it was not easy. She had stabilized at a bottle of wine on Friday and Saturday evenings with a meal with her partner. It has been like this for most of the year. Three weeks ago Linda was in the supermarket doing some shopping and bought a bottle of vodka, took it home, and secretly drank it. She has continued with a daily intake of vodka; the last few days it has been half a bottle a day. She feels she has really blown it and gone back to the way she was. Linda is feeling low.*

Clearly, Linda had been achieving her goal, but she has relapsed back to her old drinking pattern. She is lacking in self-belief and initially will need a lot of time to talk, to be heard, and to experience being warmly accepted as she is in the present. Within her there will still exist a motivation to control her alcohol use; however, at the moment this has become submerged. Being allowed to describe all that is present within her, Linda is likely to move towards reconnecting with the motivation that had kept her drinking under control for many months although she may need to break through the 'alcohol barrier' (a lowering of mood and motivation) to do so. It will be a sensitive time for her: the depth of shame can be intense and the difficulty in voicing what has happened and what she feels very real. Time, availability and a set of feelings feeding into low self-worth can make alcohol an attractive coping mechanism.

> *Linda:* I'm so ashamed; I can't even look you in the eye. I really didn't want to come today.

> *Counsellor:* It was hard for you to come here, but I am feeling really glad that you have.

> *Linda:* It's the shame, I just wanted to hide it, from me, you, everyone. It's awful. Yet I've managed to get here. I've already had a drink today.

> *Counsellor:* The shame is overwhelming, you've got here but you really want to hide away.

> *Linda:* I still do; yet I also have to face it.

> *Counsellor:* Face the shame.

> *Linda (after long silence):* It's hard to be me at the moment.

> *Counsellor:* Really hard.

> *Linda (after another long silence):* You're not reacting how I expected.

> *Counsellor:* Not reacting how you expected? You seem surprised?

> *Linda:* I expected you to be angry. Well, somehow I knew you wouldn't, but then I also expected it. Everyone else gets angry when I drink.

> *Counsellor:* You really are used to getting anger in response to drinking?

> *Linda:* Yes. But this feels different.

> *Counsellor:* Feels different?

Linda is opening up to a new experience, and is offered an opportunity to explore how it feels, what it means to her. She is getting an empathic response within an atmosphere of positive regard and it is challenging her concept of herself. She is not being condemned for her relapse. She is confused, yet she is likely to gain strength from the counsellor's quiet and warm acceptance.

Time to reflect and make sense of it all is needed, preferably soon after the event, though this is not always feasible. Exploring and contrasting Linda's responses to angry or accepting reactions from others is likely to be helpful. She will seek that which is most satisfying to her, and realize she has options other than to live out the old pattern of using alcohol to cope with negative judgements. Her locus of evaluation which has been invested in the angry reactions of others in the past and in an expectation of criticism, is being offered an opportunity to shift to a more internal focus. Slowly, greater resilience can emerge. Sensing that her shame is heard allows her to move on, to explore the possibility of being more or other than her 'shamed self'.

Linda's next challenge may be her feeling of being 'back at square one', or of 'letting the counsellor down'. A dialogue may develop along the following lines:

Linda: I feel as though I'm back to where I started, out of control again, unable to stop myself.

Counsellor: As though you've lost all that you have gained?

Linda: Yes. I thought I was OK. I really thought everything was fine. I never expected to be back where I am – and drinking secretly as well.

Counsellor: You really thought you had it under control, and the secretiveness seems so difficult to accept.

Linda: Yes. What am I doing to myself? I've got to turn this around. I don't know what came over me.

Counsellor: It seems to me that we have two directions here, to explore the trigger for the drinking to help you understand what came over you, or to focus on ways of turning around the current alcohol intake.

Linda: I've let you down, haven't I? All that planning.

Counsellor: I feel sad that it has happened, but I do not feel let down.

(*Note the subtle difference between feeling disappointed for the client and feeling personally let down. It is a human response to feel sorry that a client relapses. It is something else to feel let down, probably reflecting that the counsellor has invested too much of himself or herself in the client's action plan.*)

Linda: I do.

Counsellor: You feel sad. It's hard to come to terms with.

Linda: I'm so angry with myself, I really have let myself down.

(*Linda is now moving from shame to owning her own anger. The counsellor has not been angry with her, has not given her a reason to live out her old pattern, and she is taking responsibility for what happened.*)

Counsellor: You feel you have let yourself down and it has left you with a lot of anger. You put a great deal into planning change ...

Linda: Yes. I know I'm feeling sorry for myself, and I need to understand what happened. I don't want to be caught out again.

Counsellor: You don't want to be caught out.

Linda: I need to make sense of it; I need to understand why. I feel bad about it and I will continue to feel that way for a while, but I also want to understand. I don't want it to happen again.

Counsellor: That sounds really positive. You acknowledge feeling bad and you want to move on and try again. You need to understand what happened.

Linda: I have to put the brake on my drinking.

Counsellor: Sounds forceful, you really want to slam your foot down on the brake.

Linda: Too right. And I need to know why I went back to the vodka.

Linda is engaging more and more with her determination and motivation to put the brake on her drinking, as well as her need to understand. This dialogue captures many of the facets of relapse. The client who has been motivated to control a drinking pattern is still the same person underneath, even in relapse. It is a very human time as two people contemplate together what has occurred. It is also a painful time.

An open exploration of what Linda associates with her relapse will be useful. Factors that may emerge might include difficulties that have built up over time: 'I can't cope with the relationship any more.' 'I'm fed up always doing the shopping and the housework.' 'Being on my own during the day at home has got to me again, it's so boring, and lonely.' Other experiences of a 'short, sharp, shock' nature may have overwhelmed Linda: bad news arriving that morning, or the anniversary of a close relative's death.

There is generally a very good reason (not an excuse) for people being triggered into relapse. As this is explored, and as Linda gains greater clarity, she is likely to acknowledge that there has been at least one positive feature: she has not drunk the whole bottle straight away and then bought another. She has demonstrated some degree of control.

NEXT STEP

When Linda came for the counselling session, she saw herself in relapse. The dialogue indicates that she is moving towards contemplating change. However, other clients may have relapsed to the point of returning to pre-contemplation, having given up controlling their alcohol use and holding no thoughts of change. What was said earlier in relation to these two stages will then apply.

For Linda, temporary abstinence may be seen as a realistic next step, with her exploring ways of putting the brake on the drinking on a one-day-at-a-time basis. Areas that Linda may want to focus on as she faces the immediacy of the next few days might include:

- Will she be at home on her own when she leaves the session, or can she spend time with someone else before returning home?

- How strong is her craving for alcohol?

- Does she need medication to stave off a withdrawal reaction if she is able to stop?

- Can she pour away the rest of the vodka, or give it to someone else?

- Will she tell her partner?

- What will she tell her partner?

- Can she take the risk of being open about what has happened and thereby break through the constriction of secrecy that is beginning to take a hold and put her under pressure?

  ◦ What are her feelings towards going back to the
    supermarket, and how might she minimize the risk of
    buying another bottle once she has stopped? (Alcohol
    is usually at the end of the supermarket aisles next to
    the check-out, where shoppers can feel most stressed.
    A useful tip is to take a reverse route, past the alcohol
    first.)

This initial period will be a testing time for Linda. She is likely
to need support, from the counsellor, from friends, from her
partner, in fact anyone she can trust. The reality is that clients
do not usually maintain change at the first attempt. Some do,
exit from maintenance, and are able to sustain their changed
drinking pattern and lifestyle. Others, like Linda, will lapse or
relapse, learn from the experience, and continue the process of
change with a fresh attempt that succeeds.

Some may genuinely feel they have done their best, and
that the reality is that at this time they are not able to control
their drinking with current levels of support. Options may
then be discussed which might include greater medical intervention, increased social support, or rehabilitation programmes.

Finally, there will be those clients for whom sustainable
change remains beyond their reach; they return to pre-contemplation; contact is lost. The hope is that, at some point in the
future, circumstances or their own growth process will enable
them to reconnect with the developing configuration of self in
which their motivation is invested.

Impact on the counsellor

Working with a client in lapse or relapse is particularly
demanding. The person-centred approach, because it is fundamentally relational, means that the client's world is making a
powerful impact on the counsellor. Intense emotions are a

common feature. The client's sense of helplessness or despair becomes very present within the therapeutic relationship, and can threaten to overwhelm the counsellor. It can be a challenge to stay with the client and to trust that the relational process is going to help the client to resolve the difficulty. Perhaps one of the most difficult situations for the counsellor is when a vulnerable client, with whom they have built a very human relationship, breaks contact without any word as to why or what has happened.

This highlights the importance of supervision, where the counsellor can gain clarity concerning the feelings and thoughts they are left with after a client relapses. They can explore how these impact on the therapeutic relationship and whether they are blocking psychological contact with the client. A question that is often worth asking is whether the counsellor has strayed from 'responsibility to' the client into 'responsibility for' the client.

While it can be demanding to work with this client group, it is also very rewarding. People do have enormous capacity to grow out of past habits and patterns when they are given an opportunity to experience a therapeutic relationship based on the principles of person-centred working. Sharing in the process of change, witnessing a client whose life was centred on problematic alcohol use becoming able to realize their fuller potential as a person, is a deeply moving experience.

Key points

- In maintaining change, clients may need a longer period of support than they initially expect.
- Drinking dreams can be a serious threat to abstinence.
- Continued lowering mood after detoxification is likely to require medical intervention.
- People can exit from maintenance and sustain a changed drinking pattern and lifestyle.
- Plans may have to be adjusted.
- Lapses do not have to become relapses.
- Clients need time to understand, and learn from, a relapse.
- Not everyone manages to sustain a change in drinking pattern.

CHAPTER 7

Bringing It All Together

In this chapter we take two situations. In the first, a fictitious family is used to highlight the impact of problematic alcohol use on the family system, and some of the issues to be addressed. The second is a person-centred dialogue with a client passing through the cycle of change. The contents from both scenarios are drawn from the range of issues that can arise; the intention is to enable the reader to get a feel for the process that can lead to sustainable change.

A fictitious family case study

Scenario 14

> *Anne and Peter met when they were both in their twenties and, at the time, were enjoying a social life involving parties and pubs, as well as various sporting interests. They lived together for three years before getting married and starting a family. They now have three children: Gemma, aged eight; Jimmy, aged six; Paula, aged three. Anne gave up work soon after Gemma was born. After the birth of Paula she took up a part-time teaching job. Peter sells computer systems and travels extensively.*

> *Anne has been finding it quite a strain coping with the children on her own, Peter being away during the week. She has always enjoyed a drink and has got into the habit of having wine in the evenings. It helps her relax and unwind. It used to be a couple of glasses; that was six months ago. Now it is the whole bottle, sometimes*

more. She often falls asleep downstairs and wakes up in the early hours.

Peter finds it hard being on his own. While he had liked the social scene, he had always used alcohol to give himself a bit of confidence. He had never really thought of it as being much of a problem, though. Since being 'on the road', and spending a lot of time in hotel rooms when he is not with clients, he has taken to having some whisky, again just to unwind and help the time pass by. He would go out and socialize but he doesn't always know anyone and so prefers to stay in his room. He drinks between a quarter and a half bottle of spirits during the evening.

When Anne and Peter are together at the weekends they have a few drinks in the evening, but neither sees a problem in it, and both assume the other is not drinking heavily during the week. Most weekends they both feel irritable in the evenings and this can lead to arguments.

Anne is unaware that sometimes Paula cries in the evening, and that the other two children go to her. They do not understand why Mummy doesn't come to see if Paula is all right. They do not like the raised voices at the weekends when Daddy comes home. They are unsure what is happening and while they know that Mummy and Daddy do love them, they are sometimes left wondering why their parents act in ways that leave them feeling hurt. They all stay close together upstairs and it is often Gemma who has to comfort Jimmy and Paula.

Last Thursday Peter came home as a surprise late in the evening and found Anne very intoxicated, having drunk a bottle and a half of wine. His reaction, after getting very angry and shouting about who was looking after the children, was to down at least a quarter of a bottle of whisky. The arguments continued into the night. The amount that Peter has been drinking came out. The children stayed together in one room, frightened of what was going to happen next.

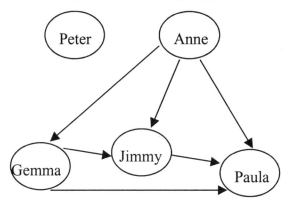

Figure 7.1 Flow of responsibility

Here we have a family situation in which things are going seriously wrong in the parents' relationship. There are risks being taken which involve the children. First, let us consider a flow of responsibility diagram for this family, and then what issues might be present if the adults were to decide to seek counselling. Figure 7.1 shows the family relationships during the week. What issues might Peter or Anne bring to counselling?

PETER

Peter is angry, upset, scared of what may happen next. He may agree he has a drink problem, he may not. He may prefer to project all the blame on to Anne. Alcohol has been important to him for many years now, providing him with a means of coping with social situations and, more recently, being on his own in hotel rooms. It became a secret habit and high alcohol intake has become a regular feature of his daily routine. The secret is out. Others are aware and he may be fearful of contemplating life without his drink, or he may believe he has a right to drink what he wants.

Much will depend on Peter's motivation for coming to counselling. It could be to come to terms with the upset relating to his wife's drinking, or the tension within the family home. He may not see his drinking as something to focus on, and may never mention it. This would clearly make him a pre-contemplator towards his drinking. In his own mind, his alcohol use is a solution to his difficulties of isolation and having time to fill. However, talking through his feelings towards his family and work situations may bring him to realize that his alcohol use is not a sustainable solution, and is in fact causing problems within the family: affecting his mood, his relationships and being likely to lead to heavier drinking and greater health risk in the future. He may then begin to consider the need to cut back; at this point he will have moved into contemplating change.

Suppose, however, that he comes initially with the intention of talking about and dealing with his drinking. It has made him uncomfortable and he is contemplating change. He chooses to focus primarily on his feelings and associations with alcohol use. The person-centred counsellor offers him space and time to explore fully these feelings and endeavours to be with him as a companion in his lonely inner world of hotel rooms. Peter is given the opportunity to encounter himself at his own pace and in his own way.

He discloses that from an early age he has used alcohol to boost his confidence, to enable him to feel more relaxed, lose a few inhibitions and become more of a social mixer. It becomes increasingly clear that he has underlying difficulties concerning confidence and low self-esteem outside his 'salesman role' and probably has a negative self-concept. Within a warm, genuine and accepting relationship he will discover a fresh view of himself, confront the configurations linked to loneliness and lack of confidence within his self-concept and begin to re-create his structure of self.

At the same time, the counsellor will be mindful of Peter's drinking and may highlight this, offering him the opportunity to explore his options, while not wanting to push him beyond his current focus. Although Peter has chosen the route of exploring his feelings and seeking to resolve underlying issues, the counsellor may still mention his drinking and enquire about it as a genuine expression of authentic concern for Peter's well-being. The longer he drinks heavily, the more ingrained it becomes and the greater the danger of dependency. The counsellor may experience persistent concern which I would argue it is appropriate to voice, in a supportive and non-judgemental manner. However, Peter may not focus on his alcohol use, although the changes within himself in response to the actualizing tendency may impact on his choice to drink heavily. He may simply not feel the same intense need as he finds the confidence and strength to seek out other activities that bring him a sense of satisfaction. This is an example of how changes within a person can affect an alcohol habit, even without the alcohol consumption being a direct focus.

Alternatively, Peter may decide to focus simply on how he might reduce his drinking, and be looking for strategies. He is probably not physically dependent on alcohol; his intake is contained within the evenings and, although it may be an established habit, he is not experiencing withdrawal or a need to top himself up. However, it is firmly fixed into his daily routine when he is away. The drinking diary might be considered as something to offer to help clarify the pattern of alcohol use and associations.

What kind of changes to his drinking pattern might be considered? Maybe regular phone calls to Anne could be built into his evening routine when away, particularly if this is part of the process of rebuilding their relationship. He may wish to try some non-alcoholic drinks during the evening, or establish a different routine, such as reading the paper in the hotel lounge after work with a pot of tea, then having a later meal to reduce the possible drinking time afterwards. If a mini-bar in the room encourages his drinking, he might choose a room that does not have this facility. He might also consider taking up some other interest that he could pursue during the evenings. He might decide to look for hotels with a health club, where he can swim, play squash, or go to the gym.

Nevertheless, feelings of isolation in his hotel room may remain, he may find it hard to engage in other activities, and so the drinking may continue. A change of job might then need to be considered. Many clients are faced with this dilemma when work situations are provoking problematic alcohol use. A change of job may not address the underlying psychological issues, but may provide a helpful 'harm minimization' response to a habit that might otherwise get further out of control in the future.

Some clients, on realizing they may have to make a major change in their lives, such as finding a new job, on contemplating the reality of this, return to tackling the drinking with renewed motivation and greater success. Not everyone has to hit the bottom before they can kick an alcohol habit, though they often need a sharp experience that clarifies in an immediate and personal way why change is more compelling than continuing with their drinking. From a person-centred persepective we might think of this as a configuration of self containing a sense of self that is motivated to change to asserting itself.

ANNE

Imagine Anne as the client, coming to the counsellor after the row and wanting to do something about her low mood and general feeling of worthlessness. She may be carrying anger towards her husband, frustration with her lifestyle, regret about her intoxication during the evenings. She could be a pre-contemplator or a contemplator; it depends on whether she feels she has a problem or not, and then whether she wants to change.

Consider her presenting herself as not having a problem, saying that it is her husband's fault for not being there to take his share of child-care, that she enjoys her drink occasionally and that it was unlucky he had to come home unannounced on the one day she drank so much. She is not being congruent because within herself she knows what she is saying is not the way it is, that the alcohol use is an adaptive behaviour to cope with discomfort, leaving her in a state that could mean the children are at risk – something she does not want. At some level she is likely to be vulnerable, hurt and anxious.

The person-centred counselling relationship offers her the opportunity to experience the reality of her situation, and her reactions to it. Anne may accept that, while alcohol offers relaxation (which is satisfying), it is also having a detrimental effect, particularly on her children, and probably on her mood. She may wish to weigh up the pros and cons of change and these considerations will become more realistic as Anne develops, through the counselling process, a more authentic understanding of herself and her circumstances and greater openness towards her alcohol use.

Anne may already have recognized her need to change and may be bringing feelings of guilt, failure, anger and helplessness to the counselling session. These may be overwhelming for her. As she engages with these feelings she will be at risk of increasing her drinking, particularly if she has learned to use alcohol to cope with painful emotions. This risk may be usefully addressed and explored. The person-centred counsellor brings a crucial attitude of acceptance to enable Anne to explore realistically her thoughts and feelings and the sense of self with which they are linked, and the choices before her.

She may seek a more strategic approach to her drinking. Perhaps she has friends or relatives who could visit on some of the evenings. Or she might decide to try to develop new interests within the home to fill her evenings in a satisfying way, or rediscover old ones that were pushed aside by the increased alcohol use. More regular telephone contact with her husband while he is away might be planned. She may also wish to have a baby-sitter and go out more. Any planning will also involve drinking some non-alcoholic drinks.

Wherever Anne chooses to place her emphasis, without change the situation is likely to worsen. As is so often the case when working with clients with alcohol problems, the focus may be split between the problematic drinking behaviour and what can replace it, and the feelings and thoughts that shape the person's structure of self and fuel the alcohol use.

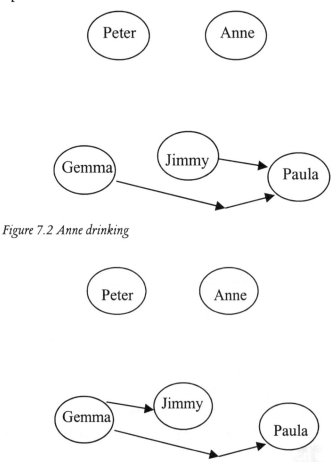

Figure 7.2 Anne drinking

Figure 7.3 Arguments at the weekends

THE CHILDREN: GEMMA, JIMMY AND PAULA

Figures 7.2 and 7.3 show what happens during the evening when Anne is drinking and does not respond to Paula's cries, and the effects on the children when Peter and Anne are arguing at the weekends.

We can see from these two diagrams the isolated world of the children and the different patterns of responsibility that are set up in the two situations. All three children are confused as they try to make sense of what is happening. They could be blaming themselves and may be being conditioned into thinking that love is partly about being hurt. They will certainly be extremely anxious.

How might the children's self-concepts be developing? Gemma and Jimmy could be feeling 'unloved' or, more seriously, feeling a little 'unlovable'. This could leave them vulnerable in later life if this self-concept is reinforced over time, to the point where they seek out experiences to satisfy this 'I am unlovable' configuration that has been generated within their structure of self, or seek any relationship, however damaging it might be, simply to get the satisfaction of some kind of attention.

Sometimes Paula is not getting the attention she needs from her mother in the evenings, and yet she is getting comfort from Gemma and Jimmy. Importantly, Paula will be receiving signals of being loved and cared for in her moments of distress, yet she is really not sure about her mother's love. Her father may become a distant figure, associated only with arguments and her feelings of anxiety and fear. So she may experience confusion, for instance, as to what adult men represent.

The two older children are learning to take responsibility. This, in itself, is not a bad thing, but if it continues they could become the responsible carers for Paula, subtly conditioned into seeing life from the perspective of 'the organizer' or 'the carer', leaving them with a dominating attitude and self-concept to carry into adult life. This is particularly true for Gemma, who takes overall responsibility for reassuring her younger brother and sister during her parents' arguments. How will she, Jimmy and Paula relate to arguments in the future? Paula and Jimmy are being cared for, so they will encounter conflicting experiences and feelings: the uncertainty and anxiety coupled with feeling good about consistently being looked after by Gemma. Gemma, meanwhile, having no support and not being able to show what she feels in order not to upset Jimmy and Paula further, will be left with strong feelings perhaps of needing to create peace, to avoid conflict, and to hide emotions that are upsetting. All will depend on what meaning the children attach to their experiences and emotions, and how this is then built into their self-concept.

These three children are likely to be carrying deeply embedded anxieties linked to their individual, childhood experiences. They may have an increased risk in later life of developing a problematic drinking pattern, though this is not inevitable. Should they develop problems and seek counselling later in life, the consistent warmth and acceptance of the person-centred counselling relationship would offer a challenge to the conditioned configurations established in childhood. The use of the 'flow of responsibility' diagrams to capture their childhood family patterns may be helpful. These may highlight problematic drinking and other relationship patterns repeating through the generations.

PROMOTING CHANGE

Let us consider how this family could change and the difficulties that might arise. For Peter and Anne, lifestyle change will be called for. They will need to work at it together and encourage each other. Initially, each may feel anger and resentment towards the other, blaming the other (which can be a powerful way of avoiding responsibility for their own behaviour). Can Peter and Anne take responsibility for the situation? They need to be enabled to communicate and listen to each other. Here couple counselling may be of value.

It will be helpful for the children to feel consistency in the warmth, caring and valuing from their parents. Fears will need to be alleviated as much as possible. The risk is that the children will carry a latent fear that it might all happen again. However, given a caring and loving environment, there is a much better chance that they will be encouraged to grow (actualize) into fuller personhood. Consistency will encourage trust towards their parents and a self-concept of being lovable. In this scenario there is a strong case for working with the whole family, helping everyone to relate openly and fully, to begin the process of re-bonding. For the counsellor, there will be a fundamental need to trust the potential of the family system to change.

Issues concerning conditioning may usefully be addressed. Not only have the children been affected, their self-concepts impacted on by events and their interpretations of them, but also the parents have their own conditioned behaviour to address: Peter's lack of social confidence, and feelings of isolation; Anne's difficulty in relaxing and coping with stress. Why had they both, in their own ways, chosen alcohol? They can unravel this and begin to realize that they have the power to make other choices.

Person-centred counselling often helps people achieve greater autonomy and self-reliance, to be able to experience themselves more fully and openly and engage more authentically in relationship with others. Authenticity will be crucial. The family has experienced the effects of secrets, of not voicing needs or of voiced needs not being heard. Genuineness and openness will help each person to feel more fully present and for that fuller presence to be valued and encouraged. A person-centred counsellor working with the family will want to hear and validate everyone's experience, promoting movement towards greater self-awareness and self-acceptance. The family then becomes a 'growthful' community.

Given a facilitative climate where empathy, congruence and unconditional positive regard are present, where the counsellor can maintain psychological contact with family members, and the urge to change and move on is present, there is every reason to expect Anne, Peter, Gemma, Jimmy and Paula to develop and live fulfilling lives as unique persons. There are no guarantees, of course, there never are, but the possibility is there. The counsellor cannot make someone grow, but can contribute to creating the relational environment in which growth towards greater wholeness, fuller functionality and more satisfying relationships may be established.

Working with configurations

Scenario 15

> *Jenny is 39. She tells her own story.*

> *Jenny:* Well I've always liked a drink, ever since I was about 14. Found it made me feel good, more relaxed, it was a good buzz as well. I suppose I'm a heavy drinker. It's usually wine but during the bad times it's vodka, or whisky – the truth is, when it's bad I drink anything. But not every day. The GP suggested I spoke about it to a counsellor at the surgery. So I'm booked in. I don't like to think of my drinking as a problem, it's what I do, and I've survived well on it all these years.

During the first session the drinking is explored.

> *Counsellor:* I know the GP referred you because of her concern about your alcohol use.

Jenny: She seemed concerned – well, I was a little pissed when I saw her. But that wasn't a problem.

Counsellor: OK, so being pissed at that time wasn't a problem to you, but seemed to be a problem for the GP.

Jenny: Yes, her problem, not mine. I really don't know why I'm here, silly really.

Counsellor: So you really don't see yourself as having a problem?

Jenny: No. I don't.

Counsellor: OK, so what do you drink?

Jenny: Wine, sometimes vodka.

Counsellor: Bottle of wine a day?

Jenny: Well, not every day, I actually have days when I don't drink and then have a phase of drinking.

Counsellor: So it's more of a binge pattern?

Jenny: That's right.

Counsellor: Binges often go in cycles; how often do they happen?

Jenny: Every two or three weeks, or so; they last about a week and then I stop. In fact, I can stop in the middle of a glass and throw it away. It's really strange, as if I've had enough. I guess I have got some control.

Counsellor: You look as if it is important to have control.

Jenny: Too right. Means I don't have a problem!

Counsellor: So you can stop when you've 'had enough'; can you stop when you haven't?

Jenny (after a silence): No. I don't want to stop.

Counsellor: You don't want to stop but can you make yourself stop?

Jenny (again after a silence): No. It just kinda happens.

Counsellor: Stopping kinda just happens.

Jenny: Ye-es.

Counsellor: You don't sound comfortable with that?

Jenny: No. Makes me feel I don't have control.

Counsellor: Don't have control.

Jenny: No. Ooh, makes me feel uncomfortable.

In this exchange Jenny has come in with an attitude of 'I don't have a problem' but is beginning to realize that she does not have as much control as she thought. She is becoming unsettled. While she is still a pre-contemplator, she could find herself sufficiently disconcerted by the idea of not being in control to start to contemplate change. Her 'I'm the controller' configuration is being challenged. There is scope for further exploration of what this means for Jenny.

As Jenny begins to accept that she does not have control, I might offer the drinking diary as an idea to help her, and me as the counsellor, get some clarity on what is happening up to, during and after the drinking sessions. However, at no point is there as yet any talk of her planning change. This is a time for exploring the drinking pattern, helping Jenny to raise awareness of her experiences and associations, her process of choice and the effects. At some point I would expect to introduce the recommended safe drinking levels to Jenny to help her contrast these with her own level of drinking. She is certainly going to be above safe drinking during a binge. In the above dialogue the counsellor has not tried to get a precise figure on the alcohol intake.

Jenny does not turn up for her second appointment, or a third that was offered. I would probably stop offering further appointments at this stage and send a letter to that effect, pointing out how difficult it can be to face up to heavy alcohol use and that the door is open for her to resume contact should she wish to do so.

Three months later, Jenny self-refers. She has had a bad time having just come out of a long binge, longer than in the past. She realizes it is a problem. She knows it is messing up her life. She is sorry for not coming back before. Jenny has now moved into contemplation. Her recent experience has been particularly uncomfortable. It is possible that the earlier counselling session had also unsettled her. It is not unusual for people to drink more heavily once the prospect of having to think about change comes into their awareness. Alcohol gets used to suppress the part of the self-structure that is developing some sense of a need for change. Jenny attends the session that has been offered and is given time to describe what happened:

Jenny: I didn't keep a diary, but the last session did leave me a little more sensitive to what I was doing. I still kept drinking in my usual binge pattern, but I felt less at ease with it. I drank more to get away from the discomfort. I had a few bottles of vodka as well this last time.

Counsellor: So you were feeling much more uncomfortable with the drinking after I last saw you?

Jenny: Yeah, and you know, it felt as though I was two people.

Counsellor: Two people?

Jenny: Well, there was the drinking me, and the sober me. I'd not thought of it this way before, but the discomfort somehow sharpened this up. It was as though the sober me was uncomfortable about what the drinking me was doing, but I couldn't stop it.

Counsellor: So the sober you was uncomfortable, but the drinking you couldn't be controlled.

Jenny: That's right. The sober me feels very very fragile, the drinking me feels strong; at least that's how it is when I'm drinking. At times it feels as though I am in a war zone, but the war is actually inside me.

This session has brought up an extremely important insight into how Jenny now experiences herself in relation to her alcohol use, and it is a common one. There is a split, part of her nature seeking alcohol and part seeking to be dry. It is often extremely helpful for the client to explore this further, enabling them to understand the features of the two sets of experiences. It can help them engage with both without alcohol and to begin to resolve the conflict between the two. At this stage Jenny has two distinct senses of self; however, she has yet to distinguish the range of feelings associated with them other than feeling strong and weak. Any further associated feelings can only be uncovered by the client, perhaps through the therapeutic process, but it is for her to establish her own engagement with what is present, to encounter herself as she is. She is then likely to move from talking about the sensed feelings that are present within her to expressing them within the therapeutic relationship.

Further sessions reveal how her drinking self stems from those early experiences when she found herself feeling good using alcohol, and when it also got her attention from friends. It got attention from her parents too – generally being told off, or shouted at. She has now been using the drinking diary to track herself closely. She has had another binge, but has kept in contact and her greater self-awareness has helped her look at what was going on. She remains in contemplation.

At another session the following exchange takes place:

Counsellor: So, you really do seem to be a lot more self-aware and I'm wondering where that is leaving you?

Jenny: I'm not sure. I find it all rather strange. I feel I desperately want to make sense of it all, of myself, but cannot seem to quite get it together.

Counsellor: You want to make sense of yourself but can't get it together?

Jenny: Yes, I see that there are different parts of me. But they are apart.

Counsellor: Different parts. Distant from each other?

Jenny: As if they don't understand each other, and as if they are competing.

Counsellor: Don't understand each other and competing with each other?

Jenny (following a working silence): Well, no, the drinking me is competing, looking for attention.

Counsellor: Mhmm.

Jenny (silence): That's me in the past, isn't it. Wanting the attention.

Counsellor: You in the past wanting attention?

Jenny: Yes.

Counsellor: Wanting attention …

Jenny (another silence): When I was told off, my parents always called me Jennifer. That was what I was called whenever I got things wrong.

Counsellor: Jennifer is wanting attention, but she got told off?

Jenny: Now she gets her attention through drinking. She still gets told off, I tell her off too.

Counsellor: You tell her off?

Jenny: Yes. Jennifer tries to be so independent. She scares me.

Counsellor: Jennifer's scary.

Jenny: I don't want to be alone. I want to be part of things. I want to belong.

Counsellor: You want to belong.

Jenny: Jennifer threatens it. Excitement, attention at any cost. But I want friends. I don't want to be alone. Jennifer leaves me feeling alone.

Counsellor: You want friends but Jennifer leaves you feeling alone.

Jenny: I used to drink to be with friends, to be popular.

Counsellor: Jennifer drank to be with friends?

Jenny: No, there's another part of me here as well. Jen. That's what my friends called me when I was drinking with them. I used to drink to be with them, to belong.

Counsellor: So Jennifer is attention-seeking, and gets told off; Jen drinks to make and keep friends.

Jenny: Yes. They are both drinking selves. There's also me, Jenny, the adult who just wants to get on with life, who has had enough of all the drinking.

Counsellor: They all seem very different.

Jenny: They need to understand each other. Jen still thinks alcohol gets her friends, but she's scared of Jennifer. Jennifer's scared as well, she doesn't think she can face life without alcohol to make it exciting. (*Silence*) That's why I binged so heavily; it was Jennifer feeling threatened by the idea of the drinking being a problem, of the possibility of change.

It is surprising how often this kind of scenario develops, and how helpful it can be for the client to identify the aspects of his or her nature that contribute to drinking and non-drinking experiences. Here, the client is putting names to these aspects of herself and these names are then used within the therapeutic engagement. Often, however, the client just describes feelings. For instance, Jenny might have introduced one aspect of herself as 'the attention seeker', another as 'feeling I belong'. When this happens, it is important for the counsellor to use the client's language rather than to start suggesting names which may not capture the experience of the client, or can divert them away from the feelings that are present.

The sessions continue and Jenny gradually forms relationships with the other aspects of her nature. She also discovers more of herself as Jenny, the sober self. Each has made adaptations to cope with experiences and to make the best out of life, but it is now clear that this actualizing process has been split: the growth process is gradually moving towards healing the splits. Fuller functionality requires greater integration within the person, providing for a more deeply satisfying experience. The counselling sessions become a place where all three aspects of Jenny can be present and find ways of co-existing without constant conflict. The warm acceptance and unconditional positive regard conveyed by the counsellor to the whole of Jenny is creating a safe and nourishing atmosphere.

Jenny remains in contemplation, binges still happen, but they are less intense now. She still has not planned specific changes, her counselling focus is on understanding herself, but reduced alcohol use is proceeding out of inner change. She does feel, though, that she wants to try to aim for a period of abstinence, and to prove to Jennifer and Jen that life without alcohol is acceptable and sufficiently satisfying. The Jennifer side of her nature thinks it is boring, but is satisfied that she might find other ways of enjoying herself. These are being planned. Jen seems to have realized already that she can make friends without alcohol. Planning for this change is most likely to be helpful if it includes all aspects of Jenny.

Jenny: I'm going to go dry for a while. I can feel Jennifer wanting to kick up at it, but I'm determined to go through with it. But I need some experiences to pacify her!

Counsellor: So what does she like to do?

Jenny: Drink!

Counsellor: Anything else?

Jenny: She also likes sparkly things and bright colours.

Counsellor: Any chance of a deal?

Jenny: What, deliberately buy something for Jennifer?

Counsellor: Why not?

Jenny: I like that idea. We'll go to the market on Saturday … yes, the more I think about that, the more it makes sense. It's interesting. I've made new friends recently, what with joining the support group and that dance class, and that has really helped Jen. She feels much more part of me now.

Counsellor: So Jen seems to be much more integrated into you, she belongs?

Jenny: Yes, but Jennifer's still craving excitement and attention, and risk. I know she's part of me, but she feels distinct from me.

At this point Jenny may explore her relationship with her Jennifer 'I want excitement and attention' configuration, learning through this how she might plan her period of abstinence more effectively, and ways of ensuring that the risk of a relapse is minimized.

Jenny moves into a stage of action planning and decides to contact friends if she feels the urge to drink getting stronger, and to give herself some quality time. She feels she could over-emphasize meeting Jennifer's demands and by so doing lose sight of what she needs. She has planned when to start her period of abstinence officially and is aware that she needs to be careful to continue with activities and interests that will keep her Jennifer self on board.

The counselling sessions continue while she maintains her abstinence, checking out that all is well, unravelling any sticky moments, planning the week ahead, and also working at relational depth to help Jenny integrate the various aspects of her nature. Part of the plan is an agreement that if Jenny does not arrive at a session the counsellor will phone to check all is OK.

Jenny is nine weeks into abstinence and she has not arrived for her counselling session. The counsellor phones. She has been drinking. She is feeling awful. It is a bad one, vodka from the start. Only two days, but she is desperate. She did not want to come in because she had been drinking. She is feeling isolated. Yes, she could make it later but did not feel the counsellor would want to see her. The counsellor conveys warmth and empathy, and offers to see her, wanting to help her nip it in the bud. Rapid response to this kind of lapse is vitally important, though not always possible, to try to minimize the risk of it becoming a full relapse.

Jenny arrives, very tearful but having managed not to have a drink since the phone call four hours previously. She is confused. She cannot understand what happened. She talks at length, pouring out her anguish. The counsellor listens, bearing witness to her story of the last few days. She eases up.

Jenny: Why?

Counsellor (after a short silence in which the word is very present in the room): Why?

Jenny: I was doing so well. I didn't have to start on that bottle of vodka. I didn't even know it was there! I must have hidden it ages ago when I was drinking.

Counsellor: It was in the back of the larder, you say?

Jenny: That's right. My friends were going to come round next weekend and I thought I'd just go through the larder to see what was there. And I found that damned half-full bottle. I just drank it and before I knew where I was I went off to get another full bottle. I've finished that one as well now.

Counsellor: So, friends were coming round and something triggered you to finish that half bottle when you saw it.

Jenny: The frightening thing was I didn't give it any thought, I just started drinking it. Thought I'd be OK. Well, no, I didn't even think about whether I'd be OK.

Counsellor: Just drank it, can't see a reason, there it was and down it went. Frightening.

Jenny: Yes, a real mix of it being available, and some kind of a need to drink.

Counsellor: Availability and a need to drink?

Jenny: That's right. Something in me needed that drink … Why then, though? Why didn't I pour it away?

Counsellor: Why didn't you pour it away?

Jenny: I didn't think.

Counsellor: It didn't cross your mind?

Jenny: No, not really. I was thinking about having these friends over ... friends over. (*Silence*) It was Jen. It was the first time I'd had people round for a meal since going abstinent. It was Jen, she panicked and I wasn't expecting that. I can feel her fear of not belonging. I think I'd got rather complacent, only worried about Jennifer, but it was Jen, wanting to have friends and to belong, to be part of things, and fearing the evening would go wrong.

This has left Jenny with her own powerful self-insight and in a place to explore, at depth, her Jen configuration, and her very real need to feel part of things. She has been allowed to find her own route to understanding what has happened; she has made sense of it for herself. This will have greater therapeutic impact than if the counsellor were to make the suggestion. Person-centred therapy is about the client making their own re-evaluations, connections and discoveries.

Time may now be spent focusing on this vulnerability. In tandem with that, there is every chance that Jenny will move on towards contemplating and planning to re-establish abstinence. She is learning from her lapse which, in effect, was a product of incongruence – she was not fully in touch with her whole self. Part of her nature that she thought was safe in fact was experiencing anxiety. This broke through when the opportunity to drink presented itself.

Jenny might have not turned up for the session, deciding it was pointless, the lapse turning into a relapse with the risk of Jenny herself returning to pre-contemplation. However, in this instance, she has responded to the counsellor's phone call, and is showing signs of learning from the lapse. She is already moving back into contemplation, having made sense for herself of what happened. She will need to formulate a modified plan to ensure that the current lapse is brought to an end and the risk of a further lapse is minimized.

Her first step may be to have a friend round to help her go through the house to make sure no other bottles are secreted in or around the house.

Jenny's awareness of the aspects of her nature linked to alcohol use will help her in her determination to maintain abstinence. Her configurational selves are accepted and are being offered the core conditions not only by the counsellor, but, importantly, also by the client. Change becomes inevitable as the configurations are redefined and she discovers new ways to belong and fresh stimulations and excitements. She has every chance of moving on and becoming a more fully functioning person than she has ever been since those first experiences of alcohol use.

CHAPTER 8

Conclusion

This book offers a human perspective on the plight of the problematic drinker, providing ideas for applying a person-centred perspective on ways of working that are in common use and have been demonstrated to be effective. I have sought to enable you, the reader, to enter a little into the world of alcohol use and of the alcohol counsellor.

Breaking through the chemical barrier

I would encourage all who in their work come into contact with people who are drinking problematically to believe that they can help to make a difference. We are all, in our own individual ways, creatures of habit. We all make choices and choose activities and interests that make us feel alive, more real, able to cope, less uncomfortable. We spend a great deal of our time replaying old scripts, old patterns, old reactions. Some are more socially acceptable than others. Some are more damaging to us than others, others more damaging to other people than ourselves. Yet we are all more than our habits. We all carry within us the potential to be more than we are at present. If Carl Rogers was right, and we are part of a created universe that is tending towards growth, complexity and fuller functionality, then within each of us, regardless of external habit, exists potential to grow through our experiencing.

To repeat the words of Carl Rogers:

> Individuals have within themselves vast resources for
> self-understanding and for altering their self-concepts,
> basic attitudes, and self-directed behaviour; these resources
> can be tapped if a definable climate of facilitative
> psychological attitudes can be provided. (Rogers 1980,
> p.115)

We can help people break through the chemical barrier that problematic drinking generates within the body. It is not always easy or simple. If it can pull counsellors to the limits of endurance, and beyond, what about our clients? I well remember expressing my concern to one client as to her well-being and how she would cope as she was about to leave an in-patient detoxification facility. She turned and looked at me, and said, 'How do you think I feel? I don't want to end up back in here again'. We can fall into the trap as I did of being so in touch with our own genuinely felt concern that we lose sight of the feelings that are in our clients as they contemplate their next step. Change is possible, but it can be a psychological roller-coaster. Are we prepared to join with our clients and share in that ride? If we are going to be effective I believe we have to be not only prepared to, but able to.

My experience of working with clients who have alcohol problems suggests that a large part of their difficulty lies with their sensitivity to their emotions. For some this is a cause of alcohol use, but it can be an effect of excessive alcohol intake as well. For some people alcohol can shut away the emotions; for others it opens them up, as though there is a trap-door to the feeling nature. Alcohol oils the hinge, leaving some people experiencing it swinging shut while for others it swings wide open. Clients often find this image helpful in enabling them to grasp where alcohol takes them, and which kinds of feelings become present or are blocked away.

Alcohol is becoming more available and is being marketed in an extremely seductive manner. We are also in many ways living in more stressful times, and I believe that while for many people problematic alcohol use can be a habit out of control, or a way of anaesthetizing trauma, it is also symptomatic of a wider malaise: a lack of meaningful existence. We are being brought up in a world that is increasingly artificial; everything is processed: food, the media, entertainment. As persons, we are increasingly chemically affected whether through the food we eat, the air we breathe, the water we drink or the materials we are in daily contact with. We find illusion and reality being blurred constantly. It is my belief that all this causes stress on our biological and psychological systems.

We each have the potential for greater wholeness and congruent experiencing, yet there is a great deal of fragmentation, incongruence and unnaturalness about so much of our materialistic culture. Perhaps at some deep level and only at the edge of our awareness, an emptiness or an isolation that comes from being cut off from our whole self is being experienced. Alcohol can then become an attractive solution, either to dull the discomfort or to help maintain artificiality. With more and more people being conditioned into heavier drinking, and at an earlier age, and with the availability of alcohol being extended into virtually every social arena, we are at risk of becoming an alcohol-centred society, or to put it another way, a chemically dependent society.

Importance of supervision

We must not forget the feelings of the counsellor and how they are dealt with. Working with problematic drinkers brings particular pressures to bear on counsellors: boundaries may be tested, chaos may emerge and be reflected into the counsellor's practice; great neediness may overwhelm the counsellor;

frustration and irritation may arise in the counsellor (which are generally also present in the client and can be usefully voiced). Supervision is a vital component of good practice.

Working with this client group is intense. Supervision for all counselling (and any person-to-person therapeutic work) is crucial for the well-being of both the client and the counsellor. It seems to me particularly important when working with clients who experience the tremendous range of feelings and difficulties that are often associated with problematic drinking. There can be so much uncertainty and unpredictability. The scale of the harm that the individual has experienced or may be causing to him or herself, and/or others, makes an impact on the counsellor. It can be extremely demanding and, while I do not wish to suggest that this client group is more difficult to work with than other client groups, what I do want to emphasize is the importance of supervision to ensure that the counsellor is functioning effectively within a client's often confused and chemically affected world.

Is it necessary to have a supervisor with experience of this client group? Many of the issues underlying alcohol use are those faced by most counsellors. The added complication is the alcohol, and what I think is perhaps most important is that the supervisor should have clarity with regard to their own attitude towards the client group. It is not helpful for supervisees to be told not to work with this client group, or to be encouraged to send them to AA and refuse to work with the drinking behaviour. Some knowledge of alcohol and its effects is going to be helpful to the supervisor, and I would personally encourage them to seek a short placement with an alcohol counselling agency to develop their personal awareness and appreciation of the world of the problem drinker.

A final comment is that counsellors and psychotherapists need to reflect seriously on their own use of alcohol (or other chemicals) as a method of coping where supervision and other forms of support are not meeting their needs. Dryden (1995, p.36) highlights that 'for some [counsellors], increasing use of alcohol to blot out the images and to "help" with relaxing was a reality' from his own research. As has been noted, alcohol disrupts congruence, and it may have a major impact on the effectiveness of the counsellor who regularly uses alcohol to avoid sets of feelings or images arising through professional work.

Alcohol and spirituality

Within the world of counselling, there seems to be growing interest in spirituality. Are there similarities between a craving for alcohol and the altered state of consciousness that it brings, and striving for what some term 'spiritual experience'? Is heavy alcohol use always a way of escape, or could it sometimes be a way that a person has learned to gain some greater sense of reality? Growth takes us to places within ourselves that we find more fulfilling and that inspire us to live in a way that is more deeply satisfying. For some the aim of growth is simple: to discover a place where there is no longer any emotional, mental or psychological hurt or discomfort, where they can feel more free. Alcohol helps them to discover this anaesthetized place where they can, in a sense, float away from their problems. Many also pursue the mystical quest for a similar purpose – to escape rather than to develop themselves as whole people. Psychological anaesthesia is not a truly sustainable path of personal growth. At best it can provide a temporary respite but it also offers the danger of becoming an addictive habit.

Surely the goal is not to escape, but to be more in touch with who we are: the pleasures and the pains, the highs and the lows. The 'spiritual' component becomes present when we are more fully who we are without the distortions and incongruencies that leave us fragmented within our person-hood.

From a person-centred perspective I remain fascinated by Carl Rogers' comment that:

> [o]ur experiences in therapy and in groups, it is clear, involve the transcendent, the indescribable, the spiritual. I am compelled to believe that I, like many others, have underestimated the importance of this mystical, spiritual dimension. (Rogers 1980, p.130)

If there is a higher power, as suggested within the AA Twelve Steps, could it not reside within us? Could it not be a deeply satisfying way of being that lies at some fundamental core of our being, yet with which we have little contact in our day-to-day experience, and which negative conditioning obstructs? Could we have potentialities in terms of experience and relationship that in some way transcend our everyday world? Perhaps, as we become more whole in ourselves, that 'spiritual' aspect of who we are also becomes more present.

The people I see with alcohol problems have the capacity to grow towards greater self-fulfilment and wholeness; the presence of the actualizing tendency urges everyone towards reaching or realizing fuller potential, to become more than the person they have been before. It is vital for the counsellor who is working with clients with alcohol problems to look beyond the drinking to the person behind the behaviour. In the final analysis, most alcohol problems are linked to relationship difficulties of one kind or another. It seems reasonable, therefore, that offering problematic drinkers a climate of relationship that is facilitative of personal growth is likely to generate constructive change. The person-centred approach to counselling and psychotherapy is based on the facilitative potency of what we might term 'right human relationship'. It therefore offers much to help the problematic drinker to resolve the structure of their self that has been maintaining the alcohol use.

Human beings are essentially relational. The person-centred counsellor seeks to offer the warmth, genuineness and empathic sensitivity that will enable the client to move towards fuller functionality as a person in his or her own right. With this comes the hope of sustainable change.

I find the achievement of a therapeutic relationship and genuine person-to-person encounter rewarding in this work: the experience of having played some meaningful part in helping someone to reflect on, and make sense of, the journey so far; of witnessing the struggle to make choices in line with a more authentic sense of self; of sharing in his or her moving on towards a fresh, more satisfying and personally fulfilling way of being.

It is the successes that keep me motivated in this work. The experience of sharing in someone's joy when they realize they have moved on; of witnessing the recovery of a life that had been all but lost; seeing the smile on the face of a child who has got back the mum or dad that they knew in the past; or the smile on the face of the person who has found a new and more fulfilling direction in life.

Of course, not everyone manages to achieve a change at a given time, and this is for a whole variety of reasons unique to themselves. Yet even here maybe a seed is sown, the idea of change, the glimpse of another way of being and of coping that one day will be seen to have contributed to someone breaking free of an alcohol-centred way of being.

Client perspectives

'I have seen a lot of counsellors with my problem and I know deep down that it is up to *me* in the end. Everyone can advise you, but you have to face up to your own problems and I have found that life has many downs and ups, but the downs still are never as bad as when you are drinking. The ups are far better than you can imagine and I know that even though things can be very hard, I can laugh and smile again, like I used to, without feeling so guilty.

'I also feel that not enough is spoken in public about alcohol, but more about drugs. I feel this is because to go to the pub or have a drink is part of a lot of people's social time and people without my problem cannot see that alcohol is a drug, but one which can be bought anywhere. Drugs are not 'over the counter' so some people think that alcohol is worse to take drugs, but alcohol I feel is far worse because you can go and get it anywhere or at any time.

'I also find alcohol support groups very helpful as I felt I was the only person in this world with my addiction, but talking and sharing with others I feel as though I can relate to all of them.'

'I feel that it is the younger ones who need help somehow. At my ripe old age (79) I do feel that the *temptation* is only within myself. This is coupled, for myself, with an innermost feeling of fear of letting down my family and friends who have been so supportive.'

'I would like to say so much, but I find it very hard to write things down. Today's society is geared around alcohol: pubs, TV programmes, adverts, etc. When people are stressed or tired on TV programmes they sit down and relax with an alcoholic drink, not a cup of tea, which gives people the idea that alcohol makes you feel better and gives you a lift, that it can solve your problems in life. Most people today use alcohol for the wrong reasons.'

References

Alcohol Concern (1997) *Measure for Measures: A Framework for Alcohol Policy.* London: Alcohol Concern.

Association of Nurses in Substance Abuse (ANSA) (1997) *Substance Use: Guidance and Good Practice for Specialist Nurses working with Alcohol and Drug Users.* London: ANSA.

Bower, D. (ed) (2000) *The Person-Centred Approach: Applications for Living.* iUniverse.com.

Bleuler, D.M. (1955) 'Familial and personal background of chronic alcoholics.' In O. Dretheim (ed) *Etiology of Chronic Alcoholism.* Springfield, Illinois: Charles C Thomas.

Bozarth, J. (1998) *Person-Centered Therapy: A Revolutionary Paradigm.* Ross-on-Wye: PCCS Books.

Cantopher, T. (1996) *Dying for a Drink: A No-Nonsense Guide for Heavy Drinkers.* Lewes: The Book Guild Ltd.

Centre for Research on Drugs and Health Behaviour (1994) *Alcohol Treatment Since 1983: A Review of the Research Literature, Report to the Alcohol Education and Research Council.* London.

Donovan, D.M. and Mattson, M.E. (1994) 'Alcoholism treatment matching research: methodological and clinical issues.' In D.M. Donovan and M.E. Mattson (eds) *Alcoholism Treatment Matching Research: methodological and clinical approaches. Journal of Studies on Alcohol, 12* (Supplement).

Dryden, W. (1995) *The Stresses of Counselling in Action.* London: Sage.

Dryden, W. and Feltham, C. (1994) *Developing Counsellor Training.* London: Sage.

Farrell, M. (1996) 'A person centred approach? Working with addictions.' *Person Centred Practice 1.* London: BAPCA.

Feltham, C. (1995) *What is Counselling?* London: Sage.

Fossey, E. (1994) *Growing Up with Alcohol.* London and New York: Routledge.

Haley, J. and Hoffman, L. (1967) *Techniques of Family Therapy.* New York: Basic Books.

Heather, N. and Robertson, I. (1989) *Problem Drinking.* Oxford: Oxford University Press.

Hoffman, L. (1981) *Foundations of Family Therapy*. New York: Basic Books Inc.

Home Office (1993) 'Possible reforms of the liquor licensing system in England and Wales: A consultation paper.' London: Home Office. Quoted in Fossey, E. (1994) *Growing Up with Alcohol*. London and New York: Routledge.

Mearns, D. (1992) 'On the self-concept striking back.' In W. Dryden (ed) *Hard Earned Lessons from Counselling in Action*. London: Sage.

Mearns, D. (1994) *Developing Person-Centred Counselling*. London: Sage.

Mearns, D. and Thorne, B. (1988) *Person-Centred Counselling in Action*. London: Sage.

Mearns, D. (1998) 'Working at relational depth: Person-centred intrapsychic "family" therapy.' Paper presented to the joint annual conference of the British Association for Counselling and the European Association for Counselling, Southampton.

Mearns, D. (1999) 'Person-centered therapy with configurations of self.' *Counselling 10*, 2, 125–130.

Miller, W.R. (1985) 'Motivation for treatment: A review with special emphasis on alcoholism.' *Psychological Bulletin 98*, 84–107. Quoted in M. Sanchez-Craig (1996) *A Therapist's Manual: Secondary Prevention of Alcohol Problems*. Toronto: Addiction Research Foundation.

Miller, W.R. and Joyce, M.A. (1979) 'Prediction of abstinence, controlled drinking and heavy drinking outcomes following self control training.' *Journal of Consulting and Clinical Psychology 47*, 773–775. Quoted in M. Sanchez-Craig (1996) *A Therapist's Manual: Secondary Prevention of Alcohol Problems*. Toronto: Addiction Research Foundation.

Miller, W.R. and Rollnick, S. (1991) *Motivational Interviewing, Preparing People to Change Addictive Behaviour*. New York: The Guilford Press.

Plant, M., Single, E. and Stockwell, T. (eds) (1997) *Alcohol: Minimising the Harm. What Works?* London: Free Association Books Ltd.

Powell, T.J. and Enright, S.J. (1990) *Anxiety and Stress Management*. London and New York: Routledge.

Prochaska, J.O. and DiClemente, C.C. (1982) 'Transtheoretical therapy: towards a more integrative model of change.' *Psychotherapy: Theory, Research and Practice, 19*, 276–88.

Rogers, C.R. (1951) *Client-centred Therapy*. London: Constable (1992 reprint).

Rogers, C.R. (1957) 'The necessary and sufficient conditions of therapeutic personality change.' *Journal of Consulting Psychology 21*, 95–103.

Rogers, C.R. (1961) *On Becoming a Person*. London: Constable.

Rogers, C.R. (1978) *Carl Rogers on Personal Power*. London: Constable.

Rogers, C.R. (1980) *A Way of Being*. Boston: Houghton Mifflin.

Rogers, C.R. (1986) 'A client-centered/person-centered approach to therapy.' In I. Kutash and A. Wolfe (eds) *Psychotherapists' Casebook*. San Francisco: Jossey-Bass (pp.197–208). Quoted in J. Bozarth (1998) *Person-Centered Therapy: A Revolutionary Paradigm* (p.6). Llangarron: PCCS Books.

Royal College of Physicians (1987) *A Great and Growing Evil: The Medical Consequences of Alcohol Abuse*. London: Tavistock Publications Ltd.

Royal College of Psychiatrists (1986) *Alcohol: Our Favourite Drug*. London: Tavistock Publications Ltd.

Stockwell, T., Single, E., Hawks, D. and Rehm, I. (1996) 'Sharpening the focus of alcohol policy from aggregate consumption to harm and risk reduction.' Paper presented at 22nd Annual Alcohol Epidemiology Symposium, Kettil Bruun Society, Edinburgh, 7 June. Quoted in Plant, Single and Stockwell (1997).

Street, E. (1994) *Counselling for Family Problems*. London: Sage.

Velleman, R. (1992) *Counselling for Alcohol Problems*. London: Sage.

Velleman, R. (1993) *Alcohol and the Family. (Occasional Paper)*. London: Institute of Alcohol Studies.

Velleman, R. (1995) *Resilient and Un-Resilient Transitions to Adulthood: The Children of Problem Drinking Parents*. London: Institute of Alcohol Studies.

Velleman, R. and Orford, J (1993) 'The adulthood adjustment of offspring of parents with drinking problems.' *British Journal of Psychiatry*, 503–516.

Ward, M. and Goodman, C. (1995) *Alcohol Problems in Old Age*. Ware: Wynne Howard Publishing.

Warner, M.S. (1991) 'Fragile process.' In L. Fusek (ed) *New Directions in Client-centered Therapy: Practice with Difficult Client Populations* (Monograph Series 1) (pp.41–58) Chicago: Chicago Counseling and Psychotherapy Center.

Warner, M.S. (1998) 'A client-centered approach to therapeutic work with dissociated and fragile process.' In L. Greenberg, J. Watson, and G. Lietaer (eds) *Handbook of Experiential Psychology*. New York: Guilford Press.

Further Reading

Alcohol

Eurocare (1998) *Alcohol Problems in the Family: A Report to the European Union*. St. Ives, Cambridgeshire: Eurocare.

Heather, N. and Robertson, I. (1997) *Problem Drinking* (Third edition). Oxford: Oxford University Press.

Levin, J. D. (1998) *Couple and Family Therapy of Addiction*. New Jersey: Aronson.

Plant, M. (1997) *Women and Alcohol: Contemporary and Historical Perspectives*. London: Free Association Books Ltd.

Plant, M. (1985) *Women, Drinking and Pregnancy*. London: Tavistock Publications Ltd.

Plant, M. and Plant, M. (1992) *Risk-Takers, Alcohol, Drugs, Sex and Youth*. London: Routledge.

Plant, M. and Cameron, D. (eds) (2000) *The Alcohol Report*. London: Free Association Books.

Rollnick, S., Mason, P. and Butler, C. (1999) *Health Behaviour Change*. Sidcup: Churchill Livingstone.

Sanchez-Craig, M. (1996) *A Therapist's Manual: Secondary Prevention of Alcohol Problems*. Toronto: Addiction Research Foundation.

Timms, L. and Barnard. J. (1997) *Alcohol Related Ill-Health in Older People: Needs Assessment Report*. Southampton and South West Hampshire: Joint Commissioning Board for Substance Misuse.

Tyler, A. (1995) *Street Drugs*. London: Hodder and Stoughton.

Velleman, R. and Orford, J. (1992) *The Importance of Family Disharmony in Explaining Childhood Problems in the Children of Problem Drinkers*. Addiction Research. Reading: Harwood Academic Publishers.

Ward, M. (1997) *Alcohol and Older People: A Neglected Area*. A literature review. London: Health Education Authority.

Person-Centred Approach

Barrett-Leonard, G.T. (1998) *Carl Rogers' Helping System: Journey and Substance*. London: Sage.

Merry, T. (1999) *Learning and Being in Person Centred Counselling.* Ross-on-Wye: PCCS Books.

Merry, T. (ed) (1999) *Person-Centred Practice: The BAPCA Reader.* Ross-on-Wye: PCCS Books.

Mearns, D. and Thorne, B. (1999) *Person-Centred Counselling in Action.* Second edition. London: Sage.

Mearns, D. and Thorne, B. (2000) *Person-Centred Therapy Today.* London: Sage.

O' Leary, C. (1999) *Counselling Couples and Families, A Person-Centred Approach.* London: Sage.

Fairhurst, I. (ed) (1999) *Women Writing in the Person-Centred Approach.* Ross-on-Wye: PCCS Books.

Subject Index

Author Index